Lessons for Welfare Reform

An Analysis of the AFDC Caseload and Past Welfare-to-Work Programs

Dave M. O'Neill
Nathan Kline Institute for Psychiatric Research

June Ellenoff O'Neill
Baruch College
City University of New York

1997

W.E. Upjohn Institute for Employment Research
Kalamazoo, Michigan

Library of Congress Cataloging-in-Publication Data

O'Neill, Dave M.
  Lessons for welfare reform : an analysis of the AFDC caseload and
past welfare-to-work programs / Dave M. O'Neill, June Ellenoff O'Neill.
    p. cm.
  Includes bibliographical references and index.
  ISBN 0–88099–180–1 (cloth : alk. paper). — ISBN 0–88099–179–8
(pbk. : alk. paper)
  1. Aid to families with dependent children programs—United States—Evaluation.
2. Welfare recipients—Employment—United States.   3. Public welfare—United
States—Evaluation.   I. O'Neill, June.   II. Title.
HV699.054   1997
362.5' 8' 0973—dc21   97–20524
                                                                    CIP

The facts presented in this study and the observations and viewpoints expressed are
the sole responsibility of the authors. They do not necessarily represent positions of
the W. E. Upjohn Institute for Employment Research.

Cover design by J. R. Underhill
Index prepared by Shirley Kessel.
Printed in the United States of America.

Preface

Over the past few years there has been a growing consensus among policy makers that reforming the 61 year old welfare program—Aid to Families with Dependent Children (AFDC)—is essential. The recent enactment of the Personal Responsibility and Work Opportunities Act of 1996 is the outcome of this widespread concern. The new law replaces AFDC, a federal entitlement program, and its companion education, work, and training programs (JOBS) with a system of block grants to states; and it gives the states considerably more discretion over the design and operation of their programs than was the case under the AFDC program. The goal of the legislation is to break the cycle of dependency by both encouraging those already on welfare to find jobs and by discouraging those not yet on welfare from coming on the program.

This monograph, *Lessons for Welfare Reform: An Analysis of the AFDC Caseload and Past Welfare-to-Work Programs,* provides policy makers with research results relating to historical trends in the AFDC caseload, the personal characteristics and patterns of welfare participation in a nationally representative sample of young women followed over a thirteen-year period, and an evaluative survey of the effectiveness of past education, training, and workfare programs in reducing the AFDC caseload. These research results should be helpful to the states as they plan and begin the implementation of the new legislation. For example, how many recipients can be expected to become independent on their own before reaching the five-year time limit imposed by the new legislation? And what are the characteristics and realistic labor market options of those who still will be welfare-dependent at the five-year limit? How helpful are work/training programs likely to be in reducing welfare dependency? How will current and potential recipients react to a general reduction in the financial benefits available from welfare? Will teenage out-of-wedlock childbearing fall along with a decline in the incidence of welfare participation among young women?

This project was commissioned in 1992 by the former National Commission on Employment Policy (NCEP), and it was completed in 1994. The research was conducted while the authors were at the Center for the Study of Business and Government at Baruch College of the City University of New York. June O'Neill, at the time, was director of the Center and Professor of Economics and Finance at Baruch College. Since March 1995, she has been on leave as director of the Congressional Budget Office. David O'Neill is currently a senior research associate at the Nathan Kline Institute for Psychiatric Research in Orangeburg, New York.

The project was originally designed to inform the potential implementation of a welfare reform policy that included a time limit on benefits. As it turned out, the new legislation features such a time limit. The report has been updated to include a description of the new law.

The authors would like to thank Neil Zanc for comments on early stages of the study, Carol Romero and Janet Johnston, also on the staff of the former NCEP, for their detailed review and helpful comments on drafts of this report, as well as an anonymous reviewer for the Upjohn Institute who provided valuable advice. The authors gratefully acknowledge the expert programming and research assistance of Wenhui Li.

Contents

List of Tables

List of Figures

Lessons for Welfare Reform

An Analysis of the AFDC Caseload
and Past Welfare-to-Work Programs

CHAPTER 1

Introduction

The growth of the U.S. welfare system has generated many concerns, but perhaps the major one is that welfare receipt can turn into long-term welfare dependency with detrimental consequences for both the adult recipients and their children. Although Aid to Families with Dependent Children (AFDC), our welfare program for six decades, has functioned as a temporary helping hand for many families, a significant minority of these families have remained on the program for many years. Increasingly, the welfare caseload has been composed of women who have borne their first child while unmarried teenagers. These women are particularly vulnerable to becoming long-term welfare recipients.

Prompted by these concerns and by mounting criticism of the AFDC program, welfare reform became a prominent national issue. On August 22, 1996, federal legislation was enacted that terminates AFDC and replaces it with a new and significantly different program: the Personal Responsibility and Work Opportunity Reconciliation Act of 1996 (H.R. 3734-PL 104-193).[1]

The new law draws on many reform innovations that were recently initiated at the state level. For more than a decade, an increasing number of states have conducted demonstration experiments and introduced more permanent reforms under waivers granted by the federal government. Those waivers have allowed states to implement changes in their welfare programs that would not otherwise have been permitted under the legislation governing the AFDC program.

The primary goal of the state initiatives has been to reduce dependency by promoting incentives to leave welfare or by discouraging going on in the first place. However, the programmatic approach to meeting this goal has shifted over time. The welfare reform efforts of earlier years focused largely on the development of employment and training programs that aimed to increase the potential earnings of welfare recipients. More recent efforts, however, began to tackle the other side of the equation through initiatives that would make benefits less generous and regulations more restrictive. Such initiatives have included limits on the number of years a family could receive welfare benefits and stricter work requirements for adults during periods of welfare receipt.

The new welfare legislation shifts considerable authority and power over welfare spending to the states. Under the old AFDC program, all eligible adults and children were guaranteed benefits (although the states determined the size of the benefits). This arrangement entitled the states to receive automatic and unlimited reimbursements from the federal government based on a formula (varying by state) that matched federal dollars to state spending on eligible AFDC recipients. Under the new legislation, the federal government instead will provide the state with lump-sum payments—block grants for Temporary Assistance to Needy Families (TANF). In addition to AFDC cash benefits, TANF funds would replace other welfare programs: Emergency Assistance, the Job Opportunities and Basic Skills Training Program (JOBS) and child care funding for AFDC recipients and certain other low-income families. Federal funding for the new block grants is set at $16.4 billion annually through 2002. This is approximately equal to the 1995 combined level of federal funding on all of the commitments listed above.

Federal grants to the individual states are based on their recent spending on AFDC and JOBS. Supplemental federal grants are available under special circumstances, such as above-average population growth or high and rising levels of unemployment. A maintenance-of-effort provision requires each state to spend its own funds at 75 percent of what it spent in 1994 on the replaced programs.

The states are given broad authority to determine conditions of eligibility for TANF grants. However, the law does mandate that all states set certain new conditions, including several provisions adopted by individual states under waivers. Of particular importance is the imposition of a lifetime limit of 60 months for receipt of TANF benefits. In addition, adult recipients will be required to fulfill a work requirement after a maximum of two years of benefits. Participants must spend at least 20 hours a week in an approved work activity up to 1999, with the hours requirement rising to 30 hours in the year 2000 and after. States are required to enroll 25 percent of their caseload in work activities by 1997, rising to 50 percent by 2002. (Higher participation rates are required for two-parent families.) Among other restrictions, unwed mothers under age 18 are ineligible for TANF benefits unless they live in the home of an adult relative or in an arrangement—such as a group home—supervised by an adult.

It is impossible at this stage to predict how restrictive the new law will prove to be. For example, the five-year limit is likely to be less stringent than it appears. Up to 20 percent of the caseload can be exempted in cases of hardship. Moreover, states are not barred from using their own funds to provide benefits to those who have reached the five-year limit, and these funds could still be applied to their required maintenance-of-effort payment.

This study examines information that is relevant for implementing and assessing the possible impact of the new legislation. Some of the required program changes, such as a five-year time limit, will be a sharp departure from the status quo. Advocates of these changes point to the beneficial effects that a "tough love" policy might have by pushing welfare recipients toward independence; critics fear that most recipients lack the skills to become self-supporting and argue that a benefit cut-off would simply lead to greater deprivation for disadvantaged families.[2]

The objective of this study is to provide information and new data analysis useful for informing three particular areas of concern raised by a time-limited reform and more broadly by other reforms. One is the extent to which recipients respond to changes in the incentives imbedded in the welfare benefit system; the second involves the characteristics and work skills of welfare recipients; and the third is the effectiveness of employment and training programs. The book is organized as follows. Chapter 2 describes the AFDC program and examines trends in the size and composition of the welfare population. We examine the extent to which changes in the benefit structure may have shaped the changes in the size of the caseload and influenced the growth of female-headed families. In chapter 3 we describe patterns of welfare use focusing on the duration of welfare participation, both in a single episode and in multiple spells, and we examine the correlates of short-term and long-term participation. We identify individuals who are likely to become long-term participants and compare their detailed personal characteristics with those of participants who leave welfare after a relatively short stay. An analysis is presented of the work experience and earnings of women after leaving welfare, and a comparison is made with the experience and earnings of women who were never on welfare. Training and other program services can be more efficiently targeted with this information.

Chapter 4 reviews the lessons that are to be derived from past initiatives to increase the self-sufficiency of welfare recipients. After summarizing earlier efforts such as the WIN program, we examine the experiments evaluating the effectiveness of recent work, education, and training programs. Special programs targeted on young teenage mothers, as well as strict workfare programs, are distinguished from education and training programs for older mothers with school-age children.

Chapter 5 addresses questions concerning the capacity of state and local government to implement a time-limited welfare reform, particularly when it is tied to an aggressive work-oriented program providing for a significant increase in the number of welfare recipients participating in work-related activities. Much was expected from the framework established by the Job Opportunities and Basic Skills training program (JOBS), created by Title III of the Family Support Act (FSA) of 1988. JOBS made participation in the various component programs mandatory and required the targeting of program slots on certain subgroups of AFDC recipients. Did the JOBS framework make a difference? Chapter 5 also reviews the various experimental changes in the AFDC program that have been made under the state waiver program during the last few years.

Chapter 6 provides a summary and concluding comments, tying our findings to the implementation and possible outcomes of welfare reform.

NOTES

1. For a discussion of the political debate preceding the passage and signing of the new law and a detailed account of the provision, see Katz (1996, p. 269).

2. Haveman and Scholz (1994-1995) discuss some of the concerns associated with time-limited welfare and the general problems and conflicts inherent in any welfare reform.

CHAPTER 2

Program Description and Sources of Caseload Growth

This chapter first reviews basic information about benefits, eligibility, and broad participation trends in the AFDC program. It then examines changes in family welfare participation in detail and the relation between those changes and the growth in benefits, the number of families headed by women, and other explanatory factors. Understanding the reaction of welfare recipients to past changes in benefit levels and structure is helpful in assessing how recipients will respond to the new legislation.

Program Description

AFDC, the nation's largest program of cash assistance to needy families, was established under the Social Security Act of 1935 as Aid to Dependent Children (ADC). Unlike social security, however, the program has always been administered by the states, and funding has been shared with the federal government. States set their own benefit levels and establish financial criteria for eligibility, subject to federal limitations and regulations. Benefits vary widely among the states. In 1996, among the continental U.S. states, the maximum monthly AFDC cash benefit for a mother and two children with no other income ranged from a high of $650 in Vermont to a low of $120 in Mississippi (table 2.1).

The addition of food stamps significantly narrowed the range; the combined AFDC and food stamp benefit for such a family was $882 in Vermont and $433 in Mississippi. Free medical care (Medicaid) for all

AFDC recipients and subsidized housing for many recipients further supplement the value of the benefit package in all states.

Table 2.1 Maximum Monthly AFDC Benefit and Combined AFDC-Food Stamp Benefit for a One-Parent Family of Three Persons; Five Highest and Five Lowest States, Continental U.S., January 1996

	Maximum. AFDC benefit	Combined AFDC-FS benefit	Ratio: combined benefit to cash benefit
Highest benefit states			
Vermont	650	882	1.36
Connecticut	636	872	1.37
California	607	852	1.40
New York[a]	577	847	1.47
Rhode Island	565	822	1.45
Lowest benefit states			
Mississippi	120	433	3.61
Alabama	164	477	2.91
Texas	188	501	2.66
Tennessee	185	498	2.69
Louisiana	190	503	2.65
Median AFDC state	389	699	1.80

SOURCE: U.S. House of Representatives, Committee on Ways and Means, 1996 Green Book.
a. The benefit shown is for New York City. The cash benefit in Suffolk County is $703.

With respect to aggregate outlays, the federal and state governments combined spent $22.0 billion on AFDC cash benefits in fiscal year 1995. State outlays totaled $10 billion, and the federal government contributed matching funds of $12.0 billion. However, total federal and state expenditures on AFDC families were about three times the amount spent on cash benefits alone, since most of these families received food stamps and Medicaid, and significant portions also received benefits such as subsidized housing and supplemental food for Women, Infants and Children (WIC).

Eligibility

Eligibility for AFDC has been based on both family structure and income. The program has provided benefits to families with children under the age of 18 who have been deprived of parental support because their father or mother is absent from the home continuously or is deceased, incapacitated, or unemployed. Starting in 1961, it was optional for a state to offer AFDC benefits to two-parent families in which one parent was unemployed (the AFDC-UP Program), but after 1990 all states were required to have such a program. The conditions for participation were more strict for these AFDC-UP families—the unemployed parent must have had a significant work history prior to application and could not work more than 100 hours in a month.[1] Although the extension of the AFDC-UP program to all states slightly increased the percentage of UP cases, in practice most AFDC families (typically 95 percent) have been one- parent families headed by the mother. Thus, the number of female-headed families in the population was a basic factor underlying the size and growth of the AFDC program.

Eligibility has also been based on two income tests. A family could not receive benefits if its gross income exceeded 185 percent of the state's need standard—an income standard set by the state for a given family size. In addition, the family's net income could not exceed the state's payment standard—the maximum benefit possible for a given family size. Net income has been calculated by subtracting from total income certain "disregards," including an earnings disregard (most recently $30 in monthly earnings for the first twelve months) and one-third of remaining earnings for the first four months, plus work expenses and child care allowances of $90 and $175 per month, respectively. An asset test has also been applied: excluding the home and one automobile, allowable resources have been limited to an equity value of $1,000 (assets minus liabilities). For purely mechanical reasons, then, an increase in the maximum benefit level, or the payment standard, automatically increases eligibility (as does an increase in the income disregards), since the income cutoffs for program eligibility are closely tied to these factors.

Program Roots

When the ADC program was first established in the 1930s, the intent was to improve the well-being of children who were caught unexpectedly in deprived circumstances because of the loss of a father's support, typically because of his death or disability. Since social security had just been enacted and all workers were not yet covered, unsupported widowhood was a real possibility for many. The ADC benefits enabled the mother to stay home and care for her children at a time when work opportunities for women were more limited than today, and work in the home was more time-consuming.

ADC was expected to wither away as social security matured, as survivor benefits to workers' families became more generous and more universal, and as women's work opportunities grew. But it did not wither away. As depicted in figure 2.1, after slow program growth

Figure 2.1 AFDC Recipients as a Percent of Total U.S. Population

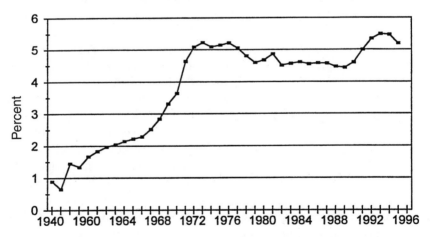

SOURCE: U.S. Social Security Administration, *Social Security Bulletin*; The Green Book, 1994; U.S Bureau of the Census, *Current Population Reports*, Monthly Population Estimates.
NOTE: 1940-1960 numbers reported in calendar years. 1961-1995 numbers reported in fiscal years.

through the 1950s, participation in the program escalated sharply during the late 1960s and early 1970s. Between 1964 and 1972, some 6.5 million adults and children were added to the welfare rolls, and the proportion of the U.S. population on AFDC rose from about 2 percent to 5 percent. After 1976, the total number of recipients stabilized while the proportion of the population on welfare declined and fluctuated around the 4.5 percent level throughout the 1980s. Starting in 1990, welfare participation surged again, reaching a record high of 5.5 percent of the population in 1993. After stabilizing in 1994, participation declined to 5.2 percent of the population in 1995.

Between the inception of AFDC and the present, a major change has taken place in the reasons for a child's dependency on the program. When the program began, the father's death or disability accounted for 75 percent of AFDC cases; but by 1969, this percentage had fallen to 17 percent and by 1991, to 5.6 percent. At the same time, the mother's having no marriage tie became the most important basis for eligibility, accounting for close to 60 percent of the families on AFDC in 1991 compared to 28 percent in 1969.

Caseload Growth Since 1960

In analyzing changes in AFDC participation, it is informative to examine the change in the number of families or cases on welfare, rather than the total number of recipients, which can include varying proportions of children and adults.

Caseload growth can be measured in several ways. Figure 2.2 plots the total caseload as a percentage of all families with children under 18 over the period 1960-1995; figure 2.3 shows only the BASIC AFDC caseload (omitting families in the unemployed fathers program) as a percentage of the subgroup of single mother (female-headed) families. Both series reveal a sharply rising proportion of their respective populations going on welfare between 1965 and 1976. But the proportion of all families on welfare (figure 2.2) is the more steeply rising series over the whole period (1960-1995), largely reflecting the substantial and steady increase in the proportion of families headed by single mothers. (As shown in figure 2.4, the proportion of families with children headed by a single mother rose from 10.2 percent in 1965 to almost 23.0 percent in 1995.)

The proportion of all families receiving AFDC remained relatively constant between 1976 and 1989, the net outcome of two offsetting trends: one, a continuing but slower rate of increase in families headed

Figure 2.2 Percent of All Families with Children Receiving AFDC 1960-1995

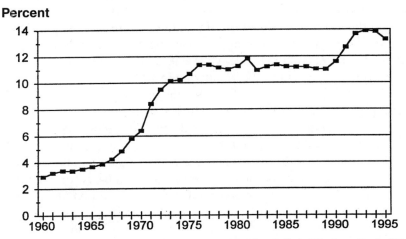

SOURCE: U.S. Social Security Administration, *Social Security Bulletin*; The Green Book, 1994; U.S. Bureau of the Census, *Current Population Reports; Income, Poverty, and Valuation of Non-cash Benefits: 1994*; Department of health and Human Services, unpublished tables.

Figure 2.3 Percent of All Single-Mother Families Receiving AFDC 1960-1995

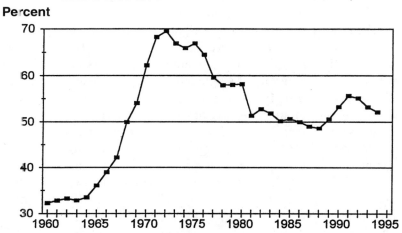

SOURCE: The Green Book, 1994; U.S. Social Security Administration, *Social Security Bulletin*; U.S. Bureau of the Census, *Current Population Reports, 1994*; Department of health and Human Services, unpublished tables.

by a single mother (figure 2.4); the second, a decline in AFDC participation among female-headed families (figure 2.3). After 1989 a rise in
both the welfare participation rate of single mothers and the proportion
of families headed by a single mother resulted once again in a large
increase in the proportion of all families on welfare.[2] That proportion
declined in 1995, however, as both the proportion of families headed
by women and the proportion of female-headed families receiving welfare declined.

**Figure 2.4 Single-Mother Families as a Percent of All Families
with Child**

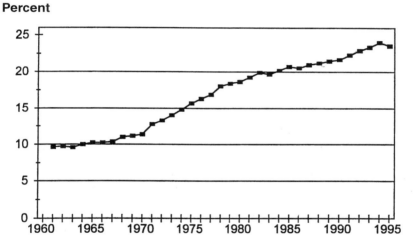

SOURCE: U.S. Bureau of the Census, *Current Population Reports; Income, Poverty and Valuation of Noncash Benefits: 1994.*

Sources of Caseload Growth

The growth of the AFDC caseload was likely to be influenced by
many factors—demographic, economic, cultural, and programmatic.
We first focus on the relation between caseload growth and changes in
the financial incentives to go on welfare, both welfare benefits and
earnings opportunities, and then discuss the relation between those

incentives and the growth in single-mother families, the primary group eligible for benefits.

The Welfare Benefit Package

When the value of the welfare benefit package increases relative to potential earnings, the pecuniary incentive to go on welfare also increases. In many states a mother with two children who could earn only the minimum wage would have to work 40 hours a week and 50 weeks a year to earn an income comparable to that provided by welfare.[3] Studies of the incentive effects of the welfare system generally have found that, other things the same, states with relatively high welfare benefits have tended to have relatively high rates of participation in the AFDC program (Moffitt 1992).

Can changes in welfare benefits over the years account for changes in welfare participation? The level of the real AFDC cash benefit taken alone increased by a modest 10 percent between 1964 and 1972 and then actually declined significantly as the states failed to increase cash benefits enough to keep up with inflation (figure 2.5). By 1994, the cash benefit in real terms was 34 percent *below* the 1964 level. Yet by any measure, participation in the AFDC program in 1994 was considerably above that of 1964.

But it is highly misleading to focus only on the pattern of change in the cash benefit, which has become an increasingly small component of the total welfare package. A growing percentage of government spending on the welfare population has taken the form of noncash benefits since 1964, with the introduction and expansion of programs such as food stamps and other food programs for women and children (for example, the WIC program), Medicaid, and subsidized housing. When we estimate the combined value of benefits received from the three major programs—AFDC, food stamps, and Medicaid—the benefit package is shown to have increased substantially (after adjusting for inflation) between 1964 and 1976 (figure 2.5).[4] Although the combined benefit declined between 1976 and 1994, that decline is much more modest than the decline in the cash benefit alone. As a result, in 1994, the real (inflation-adjusted) value of the combined benefit package remained 60 percent *above* the level of benefits provided in 1964 when benefits were largely confined only to the cash component.

Figure 2.5 Annual Benefits for a Family of Four (1995 $)

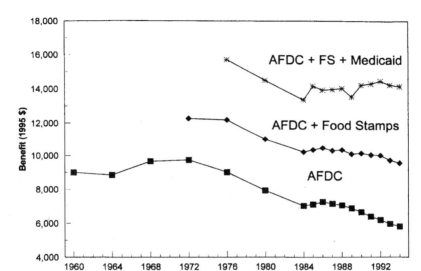

The combined welfare benefit package would seem to be a more appropriate measure for judging the gain from going on welfare than the cash component alone (see note 3). And over the past thirty years taken as a whole, changes in welfare participation have roughly corresponded with the change in the total benefit package, although the relation is stronger between 1964 and 1976 than in the period thereafter.

The Role of Earnings Opportunities

Opportunities for earning an income off welfare also contribute to the financial incentive to go on welfare and, therefore, should be taken into account. We show earnings trends of women and men, 25-34 years of age, with and without high school diplomas, since a large proportion of AFDC participants do not go beyond high school (figure 2.6). Male earnings trends are shown because they help reflect the potential income women may receive from marriage. As depicted, the earnings of 25-34-year-old men, at or below the high school level, have declined significantly in real terms since the late 1970s. The earnings of women in these age-education groupings remained fairly constant until the late 1980s, but declined somewhat during the 1990-92 recession.

Figure 2.6 Median Annual Earnings of Year-Round, Full-Time Workers, 25-34 Years Old (1995 $)

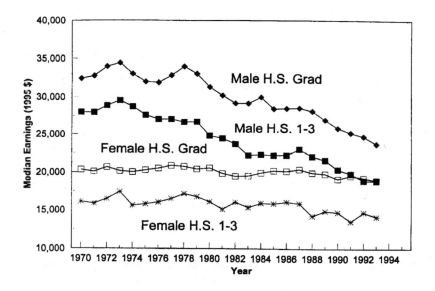

As a consequence of the sharp decline in men's earnings, the combined AFDC benefit level rose relative to men's earnings in the 1980s (figure 2.7). That factor may have contributed to the increase in female-headed families in the 1980s and to the steady level of AFDC participation measured as a percent of all families with children (figure 2.2), even though the level of the total benefit package declined modestly. Benefits declined as a percentage of women's earnings (figure 2.8) through the mid 1980s, but rose relative to their earnings in the late 1980s through the early 1990s. The rise in this ratio also may have contributed to the rise in single-parent families, as well as in welfare par-

**Figure 2.7 AFDC and Food Stamp Benefits as a Share of Median
Earnings of Males**

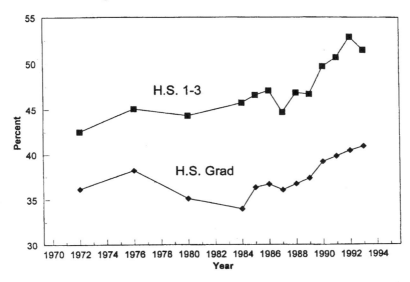

**Figure 2.8 AFDC and Food Stamp Benefits as a Share of Median
Earnings of Females**

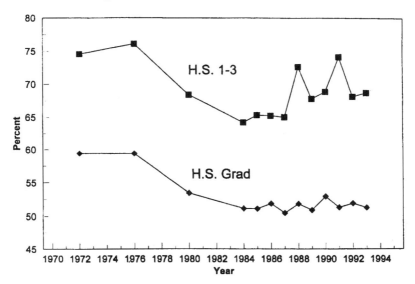

ticipation, particularly among high school dropouts for whom these benefits-to-earnings patterns were more pronounced.

Have Welfare Benefits Influenced the Rise in Single-Mother Families?

The significant growth in female-headed families (figure 2.4) has been the main source of any increase in the AFDC caseload since 1970, as the AFDC participation rate among female-headed families has declined for much of that time (figure 2.3). An important question then is whether the increase in families headed by a single mother has itself been motivated by the growth in welfare benefits or, alternatively, has been an entirely independent phenomenon unrelated to the welfare program.

There are theoretical grounds for believing that increases in welfare income would have a positive effect on the formation of female-headed families, since the availability of benefits enables a woman to support her children outside marriage and without working. However, the strength of the effect would depend on the amount of income provided by welfare compared to the income attainable off welfare—through marriage and/or work, as well as individual attitudes toward welfare recipiency.[5]

The existing social science literature, however, has not provided a clear answer to the question of whether increases in the value of the welfare benefit package influence out-of-wedlock childbearing and other behaviors associated with the formation in female-headed families. Summing up the results of seventy-one studies of the effects of welfare on marriage and fertility, Robert A. Moffitt (1996) has recently concluded:

> The research literature on the effects of welfare on marriage and fertility contains a large number of studies. The studies use a wide variety of methodologies and data sets and cover different time periods over the last thirty years. Unfortunately, aside from a few patterns that have been established, the findings of the studies are extremely diverse, ranging from findings of no effect of welfare to findings of strong negative effects of welfare on marriage and positive effects on fertility, particularly nonmarital (Summary, p. i).

Moffitt notes, however, that while studies from the 1970s found little or no evidence of an effect of welfare on marriage and out-of-wedlock childbearing, more recent studies have arrived at a "rough consensus" supporting an effect, although the magnitude of such an effect varies among the studies.

Of course, the relative generosity of welfare benefits is not the only factor influencing the formation of single-mother families. Another causal factor that is likely to have increased in significance over the past two decades is the growing ability of women to support themselves through work. The increases in women's skills and work participation and the rise in women's earnings relative to men's may have primarily reduced fertility and delayed marriage, but also may have contributed to the rise in female-headed families by enabling women to be economically independent. Women with relatively high earnings are less likely to go on welfare, however, although the existence of welfare could provide an insurance safety net. Thus it should not be expected that welfare participation and female-headed families would rise and fall in tandem, even if the availability and generosity of welfare was a significant factor influencing the level of female-headed families among women with poor earnings prospects.

The observation has been made that welfare cannot account for the rise in female-headed families that occurred between 1970 and the late 1980s, since caseload growth leveled off after 1975 while the total number of families headed by women continued to rise rapidly. The caseload, however, was undergoing a significant compositional change during this period, as the subgroup of women who had never married comprised an increasingly large share of the AFDC caseload, rising from about one-third in 1975 to about 58 percent in 1988. In consequence, while the total number of AFDC families increased only slightly between 1975 and 1988, the number of AFDC families headed by a woman whose children were born out-of-wedlock almost doubled. Presumably, that rise in never-married mothers on AFDC was offset by declining participation of formerly-married female heads. The rise in earnings opportunities for women with higher levels of skill would help explain the participation decline for this group.

The Role of Program Changes

Changes in the rules governing earnings disregards have also had an impact on AFDC caseload trends, although the intended objective to increase work incentives has not always been the result. Consequently, government policy on this issue has changed sharply over time.

As part of the Work Incentive program (WIN) enacted in 1967, monetary work incentives (the earnings disregards) were introduced. These incentive provisions changed the AFDC benefit formula to allow recipients who worked to keep a larger share of their benefits as their earnings increased than was possible under earlier programs.[6] The objective of this so-called "30 and a third" provision was to encourage welfare mothers to increase their work effort and, as a result, "to work their way off welfare." Yet the proportion of AFDC mothers who worked from 1961 to 1975—the period spanning before and after the 1967 "incentive provisions"—changed little, fluctuating between 15 and 16 percent (Council of Economic Advisers, 1976, p. 99 and table 2.2 in the text below.

In other respects, the WIN earnings disregard provision may have indirectly reduced work effort and increased the AFDC caseload. By enhancing the income attainable from welfare, it reduced the incentive to leave welfare completely. Moreover, welfare was made accessible to a new group of women whose higher earnings previously would have made them ineligible (see chapter 5 for a detailed analysis). The WIN disregards appear to have increased the AFDC caseload. At the same time, the work participation of women receiving AFDC remained considerably below that of single mothers not participating in the program. As shown in table 2.2, in 1975 only 16 percent of AFDC mothers worked compared to 32 percent of all never-married mothers, 57 percent of all mothers who were divorced or separated, and 41 percent of married mothers.

The Omnibus Budget Reconciliation Act of 1981 (OBRA) essentially removed the earnings disregard provisions in the AFDC program that had been introduced by WIN, although they were later partially restored in 1984 and 1988 legislation.[7] In addition, states were prohibited from paying AFDC benefits to any family with income exceeding 150 percent of a state's standard of need (raised to a threshold of 185 percent by the 1984 legislation). These changes reduced the amount a person could earn and still remain on AFDC. Studies have shown that the OBRA caps and the repeal of the disregards played a significant role in reducing the caseload at the national level, as well as in certain states (O'Neill 1990a; Peskin, Topogna, and Marcotte 1992). Thus,

OBRA was a contributing factor to the observed modest caseload decline in the 1980s.

Table 2.2 Employed Mothers as a Percentage of All Mothers (with Children under 18), by Marital Status and for AFDC Participants, 1975-1992

Year	Married, spouse present	Never married	Divorced, separated, widowed	AFDC mothers
1975	40.5	32.1	56.8	16
1980	50.9	39.9	63.0	n.a.
1981	52.1	38.3	62.9	14
1982	51.6	36.2	61.9	7
1983	52.4	34.5	58.4	5
1984	54.9	36.3	62.8	5
1985	56.8	39.2	63.0	n.a.
1986	57.6	37.8	65.6	6
1987	60.4	40.2	66.2	6
1988	61.9	40.2	65.9	6
1989	63.1	43.1	65.9	6
1990	63.5	45.1	67.9	7
1991	63.2	44.0	66.1	n.a.
1992	63.9	43.4	65.3	6

SOURCE: Percentage employed by marital status is derived from unpublished data from the Bureau of Labor Statistics. The employment of AFDC mothers is from U.S. House of Representatives, Committee on Ways and Means, *Green Book 1992* and *1994*.

The effects of OBRA on women's work participation are complex. OBRA reduced the caseload, thereby increasing the number of women in the population who are likely to work; at the same time it reduced work participation among AFDC recipients (table 2.2). The net outcome of these effects is ambiguous.

Recent Caseload Developments

The prolonged economic downturn that started after 1989 may have had a particularly severe impact on young, low-skilled workers, and these effects would not be adequately captured by the earnings' series that refer to full-time, year-round workers. In a detailed study of the determinants of caseload change, a Congressional Budget Office (CBO) study (Peskin 1993) estimated that about one-quarter of the caseload increase between 1989 and 1992 could be attributed to sagging employment and rising unemployment. The CBO also estimated that one-half of the recent increase in the size of the AFDC caseload could be attributed to increases in female-headed families. However, as discussed above, changes in the number of female-headed families itself is likely to respond to changes in earnings opportunities off welfare and benefits on welfare. Consequently, it is difficult to determine how much of the caseload growth is really explained by economic factors versus growth in female-headed families.

About 15 percent of recent caseload growth is unexplained by the CBO model. Among the factors that could have contributed to this growth but are difficult to quantify, are several policy changes cited in the CBO report. One factor is the impact of the Immigration Reform and Control Act of 1986 (IRCA), which legalized 2.6 million undocumented aliens. Although the Act instituted a five-year waiting period for AFDC eligibility following legalization, it appears that after 1987, some aliens began to claim benefits for their children born in the United States, since they themselves no longer faced deportation by making their presence known to the government. Moreover, the five-year waiting period would have ended in the spring of 1992 for many aliens, thereby making a large new population group eligible for benefits.

A second policy change that coincided with the recent surge in caseload growth is the implementation of the Family Support Act of 1988. Although the JOBS component of the Act (the Job Opportunities and Basic Skills training program) was expected to help reduce the AFDC caseload, it is possible that it actually increased the caseload in the short run by delaying the exit of those engaged in training. Moreover, the provision of transitional benefits (subsidized child care and Medicaid) for a twelve-month period after leaving AFDC may have made

AFDC more attractive to some individuals, thereby increasing program entry rates.

By the end of 1994 and throughout 1995, the AFDC caseload declined both in absolute terms and as a percentage of families, no matter how defined. Preliminary data show a continuing decline in the first half of 1996.

No doubt the decline is related to recovery from the recession of the early 1990s and the accompanying sharp drop in unemployment, although other factors may also be relevant. For example, in the past few years (prior to the passage of welfare reform) many states have adopted measures making welfare less generous and harder to get, or have conducted other reform initiatives under waivers granted by the Department of Health and Human Services. However, evaluations of these efforts are not yet available. The 1996 welfare reform legislation went into effect at the end of 1996, and states are only beginning to restructure their programs in response to the legislation. Although the new regime is likely to result in further reductions in caseload, it is impossible at this time to predict the long-run effects of the new law with any precision.

Other recent programmatic changes that enhance the disposable incomes of low-wage workers may also help to reduce the welfare caseload. The earned income tax credit (EITC), which provides a refundable tax credit for low-wage earners, has been liberalized. In addition, Medicaid has been extended to pregnant women and children in low-income families not on AFDC.

NOTES

1. A number of states have obtained waivers under JOBS to experiment with dropping the work history requirement for married couples with children and unemployed parents. (See chapter 5.)

2. Since 1980, the unemployed parent component of AFDC (AFDC-UP) has tended to increase somewhat faster than the BASIC (single mother) component, further causing the total caseload (BASIC plus AFDC-UP) to rise faster than the BASIC component alone. Effective October 1990, under the Family Support Act of 1988, all states were required to have an AFDC-UP program for two-parent families. AFDC-UP accounted for 6.8 percent of all AFDC cases in 1992 and 7.6 percent in 1994, reflecting a rise from 5.1 percent in 1989. Based on past cyclical behavior of the AFDC-UP caseload, the recent rise appears to be more the result of higher unemployment than the result of the extension of eligibility.

3. In 1993, sixteen states paid to a single-parent family with two children and no earnings a combined AFDC and food stamp benefit that exceeded $700 a month or $8.400 per year. If a

mother worked 2,000 hours per year (an unusually heavy work schedule for a mother with young children) she would earn $8,500 if paid at the minimum hourly wage of $4.25. Although she would be eligible for the earned income tax credit (EITC) and a smaller food stamp benefit, she would pay social security taxes and incur child care, transportation and other work expenses, and she would have less access to medical benefits and subsidized housing than a welfare mother.

4. Data for the combined AFDC-food stamp benefit level (for a family of four with no other income) are from U.S. House of Representatives, Committee on Ways and Means, 1992, and unpublished data, expressed in 1995 dollars using the CPI-XI. The value of Medicaid was obtained using program data on Medicaid expenditures for AFDC cash recipients (children and adults separately). These data were adjusted to exclude disproportionate share expenditures (DSH) and to include payments made to HMOs for AFDC recipients. Total adjusted payments were divided by the average monthly number of AFDC adult and child recipients to obtain an approximation of the insurance value of Medicaid per adult and per child. We assumed that this insurance value or "market value" measured the value of medicaid coverage to AFDC recipients. A more precise measure is "recipient value," and it is usually somewhat less than the market value of an in-kind benefit. However, recipient value is very difficult to measure empirically.

The total family benefit is for the more typical family of one adult and two children. Since the charge for a family premium for health insurance usually is constant across families with varying numbers of children, the benefit for the family of three was also used for the family of four in our example. In 1994, the estimated premium for such a family was $4,460. This is close to the low end of costs for a comprehensive HMO policy including the combined employer and employee shares. Medicaid covers drugs and frequently dental and optical services, which are often excluded from standard health insurance. It is, however, difficult to compare the level and quality of care provided by medicaid with that of private health care. The estimated Medicaid benefit for the years 1976-1994 is expressed in 1995 dollars using the PCE deflator for services. The deflator for medical services was not used because of the likely substantial overstatement of medical inflation in the data due to failure to adjust for quality changes in medical care.

5. The theoretical framework for analyzing family behavior in the context of the gains for marriage versus alternatives (e.g., welfare) derives from Gary S. Becker. See Becker (1981).

6. Prior to the 1967 Amendments, earned income in many states was subject to an implicit 100 percent tax—a mother lost one dollar in welfare benefits for each dollar earned. Under the WIN "income disregard" provisions, a recipient lost nothing in welfare payments until she earned at least $30 per month (after deducting child care costs and other work-related expenses), and then her welfare payment was reduced by only 66 cents for every dollar earned beyond $30 per month.

7. Some states have received federal waivers in their operation of education and training programs, allowing them to experiment with more generous provisions of earnings disregards. (See chapter 5.)

CHAPTER 3

Patterns of Welfare and Work Participation and Their Correlates

This chapter analyzes recent patterns of welfare use and work participation among young mothers (through their early thirties) and the characteristics associated with the different patterns observed. Among the topics addressed are: the factors associated with both the incidence of welfare participation and the duration of time spent on welfare; differences in the characteristics of short-term and long-term participants; the work experience, earnings, and incomes of those who leave welfare; and the potential market earnings of those who stay on welfare.

The analysis also provides information on the characteristics of those who are most likely to encounter difficulties in leaving welfare. Specifically, we describe the characteristics of those who stay on welfare for short and long periods under the current system. Although it is anticipated that the imposition of a time-limited welfare reform will change the motivation, and therefore the welfare and work patterns, of those who go on welfare, the extent of those changes is not known with any certainty.

We utilize two data sources in this chapter. The first is the Current Population Survey (CPS), which every March collects supplementary information identifying persons who received AFDC during the preceding calendar year. This is a large national sample of the U.S. population, and detail is provided on the characteristics of individuals and their families and households. However, receipt of AFDC benefits is believed to be underreported by the CPS, particularly among those who received benefits for only a portion of the year or who were no longer recipients as of the March survey date (Goudreau, Oberheu, and Denton 1984). Appendix A compares CPS and official caseload estimates of AFDC recipients and examines reasons for the differences in estimates.

Our major data source is the National Longitudinal Survey of Youth (NLSY)—a microdata file of approximately 10,000 civilian men and women, first interviewed in 1979 when they were 14 to 22 years of age and reinterviewed each year. We include survey results for women through 1992 when they had reached ages 27 to 35. Thus the survey follows young women over a period of their life cycle when many types of dysfunctional behaviors develop, including early out-of-wedlock births and welfare dependency. The NLSY provides information on these and many other characteristics, such as parental background, schooling, and, what is particularly unique, academic achievement measured by the youth's score on the Armed Forces Qualifying Test (AFQT), which was administered to all respondents.

Overview of Welfare Participation

We start with a summary table showing CPS data on the proportion of women who have a child under age 18, the proportion of mothers who are not currently married, and the incidence of AFDC receipt among two cross sections of women ages 16-49, one taken in 1987 and the other in 1992 (table 3.1).[1]

Only a small percentage of women ages 16-49 in the population are heads of AFDC families (4.1 percent in 1987, 4.5 percent in 1992). However, to fit into this category, a woman must be a mother and be without the support of a husband. In 1992, 51 percent of all women ages 16-49 were mothers of children under the age of 18 years. Of these, 27 percent were single (i.e., never-married, divorced, separated, or widowed). As shown in table 3.1, close to 9 percent of all mothers and one-third of single mothers headed AFDC families in 1992.

Welfare receipt is strongly related to age, with women in their twenties having the highest incidence. In 1992, 7.4 percent of all women ages 20-24 received AFDC, compared to 3.5 percent of those at ages 35-39. The proportion of women who have children is still low at ages 20-24 (only 30 percent have children compared to 74 percent at ages 35-39). But those who do have children are more likely to be single

Table 3.1 Percentage of Women who have Children under Age 18, Mothers who are Single, and the Receipt of AFDC, 1987 and 1992; Women 16-49 Years of Age

| Age | Women with children under 18 as percent of all women | | Single mothers as a percent of all mothers | | Percent receiving AFDC | | | | | |
| | | | | | Of all women | | Of all mothers | | Of all single mothers | |
	1987	1992	1987	1992	1987	1992	1987	1992	1987	1992
16-19	7.9	8.6	68.2	70.8	1.9	2.5	23.4	29.7	34.4	42.0
20-24	30.6	30.5	38.9	46.7	6.0	7.4	19.7	24.3	50.6	52.1
25-29	55.5	55.0	26.5	32.1	6.0	7.6	10.9	13.9	41.1	43.3
30-34	72.0	70.1	21.9	24.3	5.2	5.7	7.3	8.2	33.2	33.6
35-39	74.9	74.2	20.9	22.3	3.7	3.5	4.9	4.8	23.7	21.4
40-49	50.3	49.1	20.2	21.7	1.9	1.9	3.8	3.9	18.7	18.2
16-49	50.8	51.2	24.7	27.0	4.1	4.5	8.1	8.9	32.8	32.8

SOURCE: Current Population Survey, micro data files, March 1988 and March 1993.

mothers—46.7 percent of the younger mothers compared to 22.3 percent of the older mothers in 1992. Young single mothers are also much more likely to go on welfare than are older single mothers. Thus, 52 percent of single mothers ages 20-24 were on AFDC in 1992, compared to 21 percent of single mothers in the age group 35-39. The incidence of AFDC receipt among single mothers increased slightly between 1987 and 1992 among women under the age of 30, but was unchanged overall as the proportion of women in their thirties and forties increased relative to other age groups.

Incidence and Duration of Welfare Participation: The Role of Marital Status and Age at Birth of First Child

The number of AFDC families that we observe at any point in time is the result of decisions made by two groups of family heads. The first refers to the decision whether to go on AFDC made by those who are not yet on welfare. (This is the incidence of participation.) The other decision is made by families already on AFDC and concerns whether to stay with the program or to leave, and this decision influences the duration of time spent on AFDC. In this section we utilize the longitudinal information in the NLSY to describe patterns of welfare use and the characteristics associated with greater incidence and greater duration.

Welfare Incidence

Table 3.2 examines the percentage of women who ever received welfare during the 14-year period 1978 through 1991 for all women in the NLSY who had a first birth between 1978 and 1984. The table vividly demonstrates the importance of both an out-of-wedlock birth and teenage motherhood as predictors of welfare receipt. Of course the two factors are highly correlated. As shown in the second row of the table, 55.7 percent of mothers who had a first child before reaching age 18 bore that child out-of-wedlock; this percentage falls to 15.7 percent for women bearing a first child at age 20 or older.

The combined effect of early childbearing and an out-of-wedlock birth is powerful: 82 percent of women who were both younger than age 18 and unmarried at the time of their first birth eventually went on welfare. Although the effect is weaker among older women, out-of-wedlock childbearing continues to be associated with a high probability of welfare use. (The probability of welfare receipt is 72.5 percent if the mother is unwed but is age 20 or older.) Still, age at first birth appears to be strongly related to future welfare receipt among women who were married at the time of their first birth. The proportion of married women who ever went on welfare was 47 percent if the mother was younger than age 18 at first birth and falls to 16 percent if she was age 20 or older.

Table 3.2 Percent Unmarried at First Birth and Percent Ever on Welfare During 1978-1991 by Marital Status and Age of Mother at First Birth: NLSY Women with a First Birth between 1978 and 1984

	Age of mother at first birth		
	Under 18	**18-19**	**20 or older**
All mothers (000s)	666	1,421	3,420
Percent unmarried at first birth	55.7	36.6	15.7
Percent ever on welfare, 1978-91	66.9	47.6	24.8
Married at first birth (000s)	295	900	2,883
Percent ever on welfare, 1978-91	47.3	30.6	15.9
Unmarried at first birth (000s)	371	520	537
Percent ever on welfare, 1978-91	82.4	77.0	72.5
Sample size	259	496	933

SOURCE: NLSY microfiles.
NOTE: Population totals and all percentages are weighted to national totals.

Further detail about the timing of entry onto welfare after having a first birth is shown in table 3.3. The proportion entering welfare is again classified by age and marital status of mother at first birth, but now the data are grouped into three narrow windows of time when births took place: 1978-81; 1982-84; 1985-87. What table 3.3 plainly shows is that an out-of-wedlock first birth is strongly associated with

Table 3.3 Proportion of NLSY Mothers Entering Welfare by Timing of Entry, Year of First Birth, Marital Status, and Age of Mother at First Birth

| | First birth out-of-wedlock | | | Married at time of first birth | | |
| | Mothers age at birth | | | Mothers age at birth | | |
	All ages	Under 20	20 years or older	All ages	Under 20	20 years or older
Year of first birth is 1978-1981						
Percent entered welfare						
0-2 years after first birth	50.8	49.8	54.3	7.3	9.9	5.4
3-5 years after first birth	16.3	18.3	9.3	9.4	15.2	5.0
6-8 years after first birth	5.8	6.6	3.4	5.4	6.7	4.4
9-10 years after first birth	5.3	6.2	2.4	3.7	4.9	2.8
Cummulative percent on welfare through 1991	78.2	80.9	69.4	25.8	36.7	17.8
Year of first birth is 1982-1984						
Percent entered welfare						
0-2 years after first birth	48.8	52.2	46.7	7.9	14.4	6.7
3-5 years after first birth	13.3	6.1	17.6	3.9	6.2	3.5
6-8 years after first birth	2.6	2.2	2.8	3.1	6.6	2.4

Cummulative percent on welfare through 1991[a]	64.7	63.4	67.1	14.9	27.2	12.6
Year of first birth is 1985-1987						
Percent entered welfare						
0-2 years after first birth	34.1	n.o.	34.1	4.7	n.o.	4.7
3-5 years after first birth	4.3	n.o.	4.3	3.0	n.o.	3.0
Cummulative percent onwelfare through 1991[a]	39.0	n.o.	39.0	9.3	n.o.	9.3

NOTE: n.o. = no observations on this group in the sample.

a. Cummulative percent may include a small percentage in categories of years since birth not separately shown.

entry onto welfare within two years of the birth, regardless of the age of the mother. Approximately 50 percent of unwed mothers go on welfare during the two years following their first birth. By the end of ten years, close to 80 percent have joined the caseload.

Among women who are married at first birth, entry onto welfare is expected to be delayed, since it takes time for a marriage to unravel. Although there is a tendency for the proportion of women entering welfare among this group to be greater in the first two years after birth than subsequently, this pattern is not as consistent or as pronounced as the pattern for unwed mothers.

A reading of these tables indicates that external economic events are also likely to influence welfare entry. That is, the high proportion of teenage married women going on welfare shortly after their first birth in 1982-84 may be attributable in some part to the recession of 1982-83. The recession may also have accounted for the bulge in welfare entry three to five years after first birth for young married women whose first birth was in 1978-81.

Welfare Duration

The length of time a recipient stays on welfare is a crucial dimension of the welfare problem, and it is obviously a key factor in implementing a reform with a time limit. There are several ways of describing welfare duration, as illustrated in table 3.4. The first two columns refer to periods of welfare participation starting from the individual's first entry onto the welfare rolls. However, while the first column refers only to the first period of continuous welfare participation (the first welfare spell), the second column includes all years of welfare participation observed, which may include several spells of participation separated by periods of nonparticipation.[2]

The importance of considering multiple spells is highlighted in table 3.4. If only the first spell is counted, about half of welfare participants exit the program within two years, although somewhat more than a quarter of the participants receive benefits for more than five years. This result corresponds to findings from previous studies of welfare dynamics (for example, Bane and Ellwood 1983; O'Neill, Wolf, Bassi, and Hannan 1984; Ellwood 1986; O'Neill, Bassi, and Wolf 1987; Blank 1989). Nonetheless, recidivism is also relatively high. If all years on AFDC are counted (from all spells), then the proportion staying on longer than two years rises to close to 70 percent, and the proportion accumulating more than five years of participation rises to 42 percent.

Table 3.4 Proportion of Welfare Recipients Remaining on Welfare Longer than a Specified Number of Years Under Different Ways of Defining Welfare Duration (NLSY women with a first birth in 1978 or later)

	Women starting a first AFDC spell in 1978-1984		Women on AFDC in 1991
Years on welfare more than	Counting years in first spell only	Counting total years on AFDC 1978-1991	Counting total years on AFDC 1978-1991
1	0.639	0.829	0.886
2	0.496	0.688	0.810
3	0.384	0.558	0.729
4	0.320	0.501	0.658
5	0.268	0.418	0.559
Mean years	3.83	5.13	6.45
Population (000s)[a]	1,506	1,506	1,275
Sample size	607	607	517

NOTE: Recipients are restricted to women surveyed by the NLSY in 1992 and with complete welfare information for 1978-1991. These women were ages 26-33 in 1991.
a. The population is weighted to reflect national totals.

Although only 42 percent of all women who went on AFDC accumulated more than five years of participation, this group makes up the majority of women who are observed as part of the caseload at a particular point in time. The welfare duration of women who were counted in the caseload in 1991 is shown in column 3 of table 3.4. The dominance of the caseload by long-term participants is evident: More than 80 percent of the women had spent more than two years in the program, and 56 percent were on the rolls for more than five years.

The age and marital status of the mother at the time of her first birth are important predictors of welfare duration, just as they were for the

Table 3.5 Proportion of Welfare Recipients on Welfare More than a Specified Number of Total Years, from Time of Entry Through 1991: NLSY Mothers Starting a First AFDC Spell in 1978-1984, by Marital Status and Age at Time of Birth

Total years on welfare are greather than	Under age 20 at first birth		Age 20 or older at first birth	
	Out-of-wedlock first birth	Married at first birth	Out-of-wedlock first birth	Married at first birth
1	0.890	0.714	0.910	0.738
2	0.756	0.585	0.717	0.581
3	0.633	0.460	0.577	0.421
4	0.590	0.388	0.468	0.379
5	0.504	0.298	0.402	0.318
6	0.408	0.253	0.357	0.293
7	0.346	0.206	0.279	0.204
8	0.273[a]	0.142[a]	0.176[a]	0.050[a]
Mean years	5.81	4.31	4.98	4.02
Population (00s)[b]	789	400	152	165
Sample size	373	116	65	53

a. Estimates is unreliable since a portion of the sample was exposed to AFDC for less than 8 years.
b. Population numbers are weighted to reflect national totals.

probability of ever going on welfare in the first place. Table 3.5 shows these relationships through the concept of duration, portrayed in column 2 of table 3.4 (namely, total years accumulated on welfare through 1991 for women first going on AFDC in the period 1978-1984). Among women younger than age 20 and unwed at the time of first birth, 50 percent accumulated more than five years on welfare and 35 percent participated longer than seven years. A first birth at an older age reduced duration somewhat, but those who were married at first birth had significantly shorter periods of participation.

Table 3.6 displays the distribution of duration probabilities (counting multiple spells), by race and Hispanic ethnicity and by marital status at first birth, for women starting a welfare spell in 1978-1984. Although duration differs substantially between racial and ethnic groups, the difference by marital status within the same racial/ethnic group is even more pronounced. For example, among white women the average number of years spent on welfare through 1991 was 5.27 years for unwed mothers and 4.09 years for married mothers—a difference of 1.18 years. However, when we compare duration across racial/ethnic groups among women who bore their first child out-of-wedlock, we find that the average years spent on welfare were 5.27 years for white women, 6 years for black women, and 5.64 years for Hispanic women—a differential of 0.73 years between white and black women and only 0.37 years between white and Hispanic women.

Although age at first birth, marital status, and race/ethnicity are important correlates of benefit duration, it is also true that other factors influence how long a recipient stays on welfare. This is because duration varies considerably among women of the same marital status, age at first birth, and race/ethnicity. We turn now to a broader examination of the characteristics of women who leave welfare and those who stay.

Characteristics of Nonparticipants and of Welfare Leavers and Stayers

The characteristics of NLSY women with a first birth in 1978-1982 are shown in table 3.7. Panel A of the table shows women classified by marital status at first birth and by whether they ever received welfare

Table 3.6 Proportion of Welfare Recipients on Welfare More Than a Specified Number of Total Years, from Entry through 1991: NLSY Women Starting a First Welfare Spell in 1978-1984 by Race and Hispanic Origin and Marital Status at First Birth

Total years on welfare are greater than	Black		White		Hispanic	
	Out-of-wedlock first birth	Married at first birth	Out-of-wedlock first birth	Married at first birth	Out-of-wedlock first birth	Married at first birth
1	0.896	0.784	0.892	0.689	0.882	0.889
2	0.772	0.695	0.708	0.558	0.815	0.669
3	0.662	0.582	0.560	0.417	0.695	0.549
4	0.606	0.494	0.516	0.358	0.618	0.477
5	0.526	0.449	0.438	0.274	0.487	0.381
6	0.447	0.332	0.340	0.254	0.400	0.284
7	0.370	0.285	0.290	0.190	0.331	0.244
8	0.282[a]	0.460[a]	0.231[a]	0.124[a]	0.233[a]	0.115[a]
Mean years to date	6.00	4.75	5.27	4.09	5.64	4.72
Population (000s)[b]	486	56	379	445	76	63
Sample size	294	33	72	82	72	54

a. Estimate is unreliable since a portion of the sample was exposed to AFDC for less than 8 years.
b. Population numbers are weighted to reflect national totals.

Table 3.7 Characteristics (Weighted) of NLSY Women with a First Birth in 1978-1982 and Work/Welfare Status in 1988-89, by Welfare Participation since First Birth and Marital Status at Time of Birth

	Out-of-wedlock first birth		Married at first birth	
	Ever on welfare	Never on welfare	Ever on welfare	Never on welfare
Population (000s)	828	274	656	2,108
Sample size	461	120	248	607
A. All women with a first birth 1978-1982				
Age at first birth (%)				
Under 18	34.5	32.5	21.0	8.3
18 or 19	39.0	34.0	35.4	24.8
20 or more	26.5	33.5	43.6	66.8
% Black	54.4	33.5	8.7	5.6
% Hispanic	9.4	11.0	10.9	7.8
% white	36.1	55.5	80.4	86.6
& not H.S. grad at birth of first child	56.0	26.5	47.7	21.0
% not H.S. grad in 1989	32.5	10.6	31.6	10.8
AFQT percentile score	23.5	34.3	32.5	47.3
% at or below 10th percentile	32.3	16.9	14.2	7.0
Months on AFDC, first birth thru 1989	47.0	0.0	25.0	0.0
% ever married	53.9	71.8	100.0	100.0
% worked before first birth	53.9	62.4	73.0	83.6
Weeks worked in 1978-1988	146.0	262.0	193.0	325.0
% worked in 1988 or 1989	78.3	84.5	81.5	84.8
% off welfare in 1988 and 1989	48.7	100.0	55.1	100.0

Table 3.7 (continued)

	Out-of-wedlock first birth		Married at first birth	
	Ever on welfare	**Never on welfare**	**Ever on welfare**	**Never on welfare**
B. Off welfare in 1988 and 1989				
AFQT percentile score	28.1	34.3	36.1	47.3
% at or below 10th percentile	21.0	16.9	11.9	7.0
Not H.S. grad in 1989	23.6	10.6	35.1	10.8
Months on AFDC, first birth thru 1989	26.0	0.0	15.5	0.0
% ever married	69.5	71.8	100.0	100.0
% married in 1989 or 1990	53.2	55.4	75.9	84.4
% worked in 1988 or 1989	91.7	84.5	89.5	84.8
No. of children	2.0	1.7	2.1	2.2
Family income in 1989[a]	$22,349	$24,860	$24,120	$36,284
Married	$30,071	$33,300	$29,475	$40,793
Not married	$14,695	$16,199	$12,144	$17,578
On welfare in 1989				
AFQT percentile score	18.4	--	28.5	--
% at or below 10th percentile	40.8	--	12.7	--
Not H.S. grad in 1989	43.6	--	27.8	--
Months on AFDC, first birth thru 1989	71.9	--	40.5	--
No. of children	2.4	--	2.3	--
AFDC income, 1989	$4,084	--	$3,520	--
Family income, 1989[a]	$10,223	--	$12,461	--

a. Family income includes the income from earnings and other sources of the woman and her spouse, if she is married. The reported cash value of foodstamps received is also included in this measure.

during the period from first birth through 1989. Panel B provides data on those who left welfare and were off the program for all of 1988 and 1989. Panel C provides data on those who were on the AFDC program in 1989.

It is apparent that women who go on welfare have been low achievers in other aspects of their lives. Achievement in basic verbal and math skills can be measured in the NLSY by scores on the Armed Forces Qualification Test (AFQT), which was administered to members of the NLSY panel.[3] Welfare recipients who bore their first child out-of-wedlock (56 percent were in this category), on average, scored only at the 23.5th percentile on the AFQT.[4] Moreover, close to one-third of this group scored at the 10th percentile of the AFQT distribution, a level of competence so low it would restrict access to many jobs. The average AFQT score of welfare recipients who were married at the time of their first birth was somewhat higher—at the 32.5th percentile—while only 14 percent scored at the 10th percentile. By contrast, the average test score of women who were married at first birth and never went on welfare was close to the median, and only 7 percent scored at or below the 10th percentile.

Although welfare recipients appear to have increased their schooling attainment between the time of first birth and 1989, close to one-third still had not completed high school. In comparison, only 11 percent of mothers who never were on welfare were high school dropouts in 1989.

Mothers who were married at first birth were more likely to have worked before their first birth, no doubt in part because they were older when their first child was born. Mothers who were ever on welfare worked less before their first birth than mothers who never went on welfare, and they also worked considerably less during the ten-year period preceding 1989. For example, a welfare mother whose child was born out-of-wedlock worked 146 weeks over this period, only 45 percent as much as a married mother who was never on welfare.

The seemingly dismal qualifications of welfare recipients could be viewed as evidence that their earning capacity is so low that welfare is their only option. But low capacity may also be viewed as a consequence of a nexus of bad decisions. An early out-of-wedlock birth is likely to interrupt schooling and detract from academic achievement, while going on welfare or anticipating welfare may compound the effect. A low AFQT score may, therefore, signal low motivation or other problems, including the cumulated effects of exposure to a welfare culture, rather than a pure lack of ability. The true explanation is not readily apparent.

Nevertheless, there is another message in table 3.7 that offers some optimism. Close to half of the unwed mothers with a first birth in 1978-1982, who subsequently went on welfare, were off the rolls in 1988 and 1989. On average, these mothers had been on AFDC for a total of 26 months since their first birth. Close to 92 percent worked in 1988 or 1989, and 53 percent were married (although an even higher number, close to 70 percent, had been married at some time). Although the academic attainment of this group was superior to that of the average person on welfare (three-fourths had completed high school), their mean AFQT score was still quite low—in the 28th percentile. Yet, their average family income was somewhat above $22,000 in 1989, a level equal to 194 percent of the poverty line.[5] That average, however, disguises some disparity associated with marital status: family income of those who were married was $30,000; the income of those who were not married was $14,700.

Those who started out as unwed mothers and were observed to be on welfare in 1989 were recipients of welfare for about 72 months on average since their first birth, a finding that suggests a large proportion of the group was almost continuously on the program. Their average AFQT score was only at the 18th percentile (40 percent scored below the 10th percentile), and 44 percent of the group had never completed high school. They also had more children than either married or unmarried mothers who were not on welfare. Because they had been on welfare for a long period, they were unlikely to have accumulated extensive work experience. For all of these reasons they would have been more likely to experience employment difficulties in 1989 than those who had left welfare.

Unwed mothers who became long-term welfare recipients comprise only a relatively small proportion (28.5 percent) of the cohort of women who had a first birth in 1978-1982 and subsequently went on welfare. Nonetheless, they dominate the AFDC caseload at any point in time, and they are a group with multiple problems.

The work-related characteristics of NLSY women who were on AFDC in 1989 are shown in table 3.8 and those of 1991 AFDC recipi-

Table 3.8 Characteristics, Skills, and Work Experience of 24-31-Year-Old Women on AFDC in 1989, by Years on Welfare since 1978 (NLSY)

	All women on AFDC in 1989	On AFDC 2 years or less	On AFDC more than 2 years	
			Total	On AFDC 4 years or more
% Black	39.1	25.6	42.7	44.0
% Hispanic	9.5	6.7	10.2	11.1
% white	51.4	67.8	47.2	44.9
Age at first birth (%)				
17 or less	27.4	12.9	31.1	32.1
18 or 19	24.0	12.3	27.0	29.3
20 or more	47.8	71.9	41.6	38.3
% out-of-wedlock first birth	61.3	49.9	64.3	68.5
% southern, age 14	26.6	32.8	25.1	22.7
Number of children				
In year entered AFDC	1.385	1.562	1.342	1.286
In 1989	2.229	1.612	2.389	2.426
% high school dropout				
In year entered AFDC	43.2	27.3	47.5	49.5
In 1989	33.5	21.5	36.6	37.0
AFQT percentile (mean)	26.0	29.8	25.3	24.5
% at or below the 10th percentile	30.9	31.0	30.9	30.2
% went on AFDC within 2 years of first birth	42.5	13.8	49.9	52.9
% worked before AFDC	76.2	85.6	73.8	72.2
Weeks worked by working women before going on AFDC	140.5	293.7	98.2	44.3
Total months on AFDC since 1978 (mean)	57.4	10.0	69.1	75.6
Weighted population (000s)	1,123.2	231.7	891.4	765.4
Sample size	530	87	443	393

Table 3.9 Characteristics, Skills, and Work Experience of 26-33-Year-Old Women on AFDC in 1991, by years on Welfare since 1978 (NLSY)

	All women on AFDC in 1991	On AFDC 2 years or less	On AFDC more than 2 years	
			Total	On AFDC 4 years or more
% Black	38.2	22.0	42.0	43.5
% Hispanic	9.7	7.6	10.2	10.2
% White	52.1	70.4	47.8	46.3
Age at first birth (%)				
17 or less	30.4	13.1	34.3	35.4
18 or 19	20.9	16.1	22.0	22.3
20 or more	48.8	70.8	43.7	42.3
% out-of-wedlock first birth	56.5	45.1	59.1	61.5
% south, age 14	27.7	37.9	25.4	25.4
Number of children				
In year entered AFDC	1.42	1.5	1.4	1.38
In 1991	2.35	1.68	2.5	2.55
% high school dropout				
In year entered AFDC	43.8	30.4	47.0	49.1
In 1991	34.9	30.4	36.0	37.1
AFQT percentile (mean)	22.2	24.3	21.7	21.4
% at or below the 10th percentile	36.7	32.1	37.8	38.9
% went on AFDC within 2 years of first birth	44.4	23.8	49.2	51.8
% worked before AFDC	62.9	78.9	59.1	56.6
Weeks worked by working women before going on AFDC	115	253	92	79
Total months on AFDC since 1978 (mean)	66.4	10.3	80	85
Weighted population (000s)	1,274	243	1,033	930
Sample size	517	83	434	396

ents are shown in table 3.9. Both tables display characteristics of women classified by duration on AFDC (total months in one or more spells). To help inform consideration of a time limit, the classifications refer to women who were on welfare for two years or less and to women who were on welfare for more than two years and for four or more years. Because the NLSY sample is composed of fixed birth "cohorts," the information shown for 1989 (table 3.8) is limited to women ages 24-31, while the data for 1991 refer to women ages 26-33 years (table 3.9). With the passage of time, those who are observed to remain on welfare tend to become an increasingly more disadvantaged group, since welfare recipients who have fewer disadvantages are more easily employed (or married) and subsequently leave the program.

The difference between the characteristics of long-term participants and those who had been on welfare two years or less is similar in both 1989 and 1991. We refer here to the 1991 profiles in table 3.9. In that year, 81 percent of the caseload had been on AFDC for more than two years (more than 24 months) and 73 percent for four years or more. On average the four-year-and-over group had participated for about seven years. More than half had gone on AFDC within 2 years of their first birth, and more than 60 percent had borne their first child out of wedlock. Their AFQT test scores put them at the bottom of the skill distribution, and although some had completed additional years of schooling since first entering AFDC, 37 percent still had not completed high school by 1991.

Those with less than two years on AFDC (with an average accumulation of only ten months on the caseload) in many ways had fewer handicaps than long-term welfare recipients: They had worked 253 weeks on average before coming on AFDC and had fewer children (an average of 1.7 versus 2.5). Yet their basic skills as measured by AFQT scores and schooling are only somewhat better than those of the long-term recipients. It appears that, as the cohort ages, the proportion of women going on AFDC for the first time declines, but at the same time, those who do go on AFDC have fewer basic skills than those who remain off the rolls.[6] Future NLSY data will reveal whether the greater work experience and smaller family size of these late entrants enable them to leave welfare quickly or whether the negative effect of low skills dominates and they remain, becoming long-term recipients.

Work Outcomes of Former Welfare Recipients

A key issue in evaluating a program that imposes a time limit on participation is the extent to which persons with the attributes of welfare recipients can actually become self-sufficient. Finding and keeping employment is one component of self-support; the other is the wage rate of jobs obtained. The two are related, since work experience and the skills acquired on the job have significant positive effects on earnings (Mincer and Polachek 1974). Moreover, a woman who stays on welfare long term will not only lose the experience she could have gained while working, but may also find that skills acquired in school or obtained from early work experience have eroded over time (Mincer and Ofek 1982). For those reasons, women who leave welfare for work are likely to earn less than women who were never on welfare in the first place, even if they had similar schooling and AFQT scores. However, if former recipients persist in the labor force, the gap between their earnings and those of other workers never on welfare may narrow over time.

In this section we examine the work participation and earnings of former AFDC participants and compare them with those of other women of the same age and schooling. As shown in table 3.10, former welfare recipients (ages 27-34) who were off welfare in 1991 in fact worked extensively. Despite their relatively low skills, their work participation almost equaled or exceeded that of other mothers never on welfare—see table 3.7, columns (2) and (4). In table 3.10, only women without children worked more, and this group not only is unencumbered by child care concerns but also tends to be more highly educated. Among all former welfare recipients in table 3.10, 81 percent worked at some time in 1991; and of those who did work, 74 percent worked full time, and 44 percent worked full time, year-round. Work participation was lower for high school dropouts, but not dramatically so—71 percent of former recipients worked in 1991, and of these, one-third worked full time and year-round. Among high school graduates, 84 percent of former recipients worked, 48 percent full time, year-round.

Among women who were still on welfare, about 44 percent reported working, 30 percent for 26 weeks or more, but only 5 percent full time, year-round. These are relatively low employment rates compared to

Table 3.10 Work Experience in 1991 of NLSY Women Ages 27-34 by Marital and Fertility Status, Welfare History, and Education

| | All women | Without children | With children[a] | | | Ever on AFDC[a] | |
			Currently married	Not currently married	Total	Off AFDC in 1991	On AFDC in 1991
All women							
Sample size	4,535	1,300	2,002	1,223	1,158	651	507
Population (000s)	16,486	5,169	8,077	3,241	3,027	1,776	1,251
Working in 1991 (%)	82.0	93.5	77.8	74.1	65.8	80.9	44.4
Among workers, percent working							
28 weeks or more	88.1	93.9	86.1	81.9	74.2	88.0	38.7
Full time	73.4	86.7	62.9	74.0	68.7	74.3	54.0
Full time, 50-52 weeks	52.0	67.4	42.7	45.1	33.0	43.7	5.3
Less than high school grad							
Population (000s)	1,713	286	739	688	866	434	432
Working in 1991 (%)	60.1	70.4	61.8	54.0	53.2	70.8	35.4
Among workers, percent working							
26 weeks or more	74.6	77.9	79.0	67.3	69.5	84.0	40.4
Full time	65.3	64.6	66.8	63.7	63.2	69.3	51.1
Full time, 50-52 weeks	31.4	45.3	31.8	23.3	23.5	32.7	5.1

(continued)

Table 3.10 (continued)

| | All women | Without children | With children[a] | | | | |
| | | | Currently married | Not currently married | Total | Ever on AFDC[a] | |
						Off AFDC in 1991	On AFDC in 1991
High school grad							
Population (000s)	7,163	1,727	3,766	1,670	1,506	881	625
Working in 1991 (%)	80.7	92.9	77.2	75.9	69.5	83.7	49.4
Among workers, percent working							
26 weeks or more	86.2	92.9	84.5	81.7	73.8	88.4	38.7
Full time	72.5	85.8	62.6	78.3	71.5	78.6	54.5
Full time, 50-52 weeks	50.0	65.7	42.0	48.4	35.3	48.0	5.0
College, 1-3 years	3,957	1,251	2,001	705	586	415	171
Working in 1991 (%)	86.4	94.8	81.2	86.2	74.1	84.3	49.3
Among workers, percent working							
26 weeks or more	90.5	93.7	88.7	88.9	79.6	89.6	38.0
Full time	72.4	84.6	64.0	71.1	67.1	70.2	54.5
Full time, 50-52 weeks	52.4	65.4	44.3	48.9	37.3	44.4	7.6
College grad							
Population (000s)	3,653	1,906	1,571	176	70	46	23
Working in 1991 (%)	90.2	96.7	82.5	87.5	74.0	91.8	38.8

Among workers, percent working

26 weeks or more	93.3	93.7	88.8	91.8	81.8	95.4	17.8
Full time	78.6	84.6	61.0	85.0	72.8	70.8	82.2
Full time, 5052 weeks	61.4	65.4	45.9	56.0	37.0	44.8	0.0

a. Mothers who were never on welfare are not shown separately.

those of the average mother, although they greatly exceed the figure of 6 or 7 percent reported to county welfare boards in recent years (see table 2.2).

The annual earnings in 1991 and hourly wage rates in 1992 of former and present welfare recipients and of other NLSY women never on welfare are given in tables 3.11 and 3.12, respectively. The former recipients earned only $12,951, on average, during 1991 although annual income rose to $16,372 if they worked full time, year-round. These incomes are lower than the earnings of all married women with children (both those ever on and those never on welfare), although the difference narrows when the comparison is made within educational groupings. Differences in annual earnings may arise because of differences in the total time worked during the year (total hours worked may vary even among full-time, year-round workers) and/or differences in hourly wages. As indicated in table 3.12, the hourly pay of former welfare recipients averaged $7.43 in 1992, only 77 percent as much as married mothers earned and 66 percent as much as women without children. At the high school graduate level, former recipients' wage rates averaged 90 percent of married women's wages. Current AFDC recipients earn the lowest wages (even standardized for schooling).

Differences in hourly pay between former and current welfare recipients and other women could be attributable to differences in lifetime work experience, since welfare recipients work much less than other women. When employment is more sporadic, the jobs held are less likely to provide on-the-job training and to build skills with an earnings payoff later on. The lower AFQT skills of welfare recipients are also likely to reduce their level of pay relative to nonrecipients, particularly during recent years when the payoff from cognitive skills has increased (O'Neill 1990b). Differences in geographic region and in the number of children are other factors with a potential impact on pay differences.

To begin to understand the determinants of the wage rates that former welfare recipients receive and that current recipients might anticipate, we have conducted multivariate analyses of hourly wage rates, the results of which are shown in tables 3.13 and 3.14. The main findings of interest are as follows.

- In addition to the education and skill deficiencies of welfare recipients already considered, former and current welfare recipients worked 74 percent as many weeks as women never on welfare in

Table 3.11 Mean Annual Wage and Salary Income in 1991, NLSY Women Ages 27-34 in 1992, by Marital and Fertility Status, Welfare History, and Education (in 1992 dollars)

| | | | Women with children[a] | | | | |
| | | | | | | Ever on AFDC[a] | |
	All women	Women without children	Currently married	Not currently married	Total	Off AFDC in 1991	On AFDC in 1991
All workers							
All women	$18,867	$23,780	$16,727	$14 058	$10,912	$12,951	$4,572
H.S. dropout	10,881	16,674	10,718	8,146	8,387	10,396	3,388
H.S. graduate	15,189	18,063	14,158	13,828	11,071	12,990	5,409
Some college	18,678	21,831	17,325	15,979	12,568	14,230	---
College graduate	27,284	30,219	23,683	19,874	12,949	---	---
Full-time year-round workers							
All women	$24,347	$27,240	$22,919	$19,146	$16,043	$16,372	---
H.S. dropout	16,680	---	14,982	12,127	13,699	14,494	---
H.S. graduate	19,836	21,121	19,735	17,862	15,636	15,871	---
Some college	23,271	24,414	22,815	21,349	17,684	17,890	---
College graduate	32,886	33,704	31,748	27,714	⌒	---	---

NOTE: Incomes are not shown in cases with fewer than 25 individuals in the sample and are calculated only for women with earnings in 1991.

a. Earnings for women with children who were never on welfare are not shown.

Table 3.12 Hourly Rate of Pay in 1992, NLSY Women Ages 27-34 in 1992, by Marital and Fertility Status, Welfare History, and Education

| | All women | Women without children | Women with children[a] | | | | |
			Currently married	Not currently married	Total	Off AFDC in 1991	On AFDC in 1991
						Ever on AFDC[a]	
All workers							
All women	$ 9.92	$11.20	$ 9.70	$ 7.86	$ 6.90	$7.43	$5.48
H.S. dropout	6.53	6.98	6.72	6.04	5.94	6.18	5.45
H.S. graduate	8.13	8.71	8.13	7.37	6.69	7.31	5.14
Some college	10.18	10.79	10.19	8.95	7.74	8.32	5.38
College graduate	13.79	14.04	13.72	11.43	10.71	---	---

NOTE: Incomes are not shown in cases with fewer than 25 individuals in the sample and are calculated only for women with earnings in 1991.
a. Earnings for women with children who were never on welfare are not shown.

Table 3.13 Determinants of Log Hourly Wage Rate, Regression Results for NLSY Women with Children by Welfare Participation over Their Lifetimes

Independent variables	Ever on welfare		Never on welfare		Variable means	
	(1)		(2)		Ever on welfare	Never on welfare
	Coefficient	*T*-statistic	Coefficient	*T*-statistic		
Intercept	1.5258	6.911	1.3264	9.724	1.000	1.000
Number of children	0.0037	0.245	-0.0183	-1.923	2.061	0.935
Age, 1990	-0.0070	-0.988	0.0001	0.020	29.209	29.095
Black	0.0574	1.326	0.0604	2.450	0.463	0.203
Hispanic	0.1484	2.741	0.1275	5.010	0.120	0.153
South	-0.1860	-5.263	-0.1012	-5.710	0.381	0.414
Urban and SMSA	0.0830	2.337	0.0804	4.132	0.662	0.705
Unemployment rate (local labor market)	-0.0011	-0.120	-0.0169	-3.302	5.934	5.474
Schooling						
0-8 (omitted)						
9-11	-0.0365	-0.466	-0.0501	-0.782	0.205	0.048
12	0.0112	0.148	-0.0146	-0.268	0.520	0.413
13-15	0.1191	1.421	0.0694	1.230	0.202	0.252

Table 3.13 (continued)

(continued)

Independent variables	Ever on welfare (1)		Never on welfare (2)		Variable means	
	Coefficient	T-statistic	Coefficient	T-statistic	Ever on welfare	Never on welfare
16+	0.2288	1.839	0.2672	4.587	0.028	0.262
Weeks worked						
1986-90	0.0013	5.762	0.0018	11.367	148.900	212.406
1980-85	0.0000	0.076	0.0004	3.256	102.517	194.635
Worked full time	0.0604	1.720	0.1203	5.555	0.734	0.799
Ever armed forces	0.0793	0.650	0.1212	1.574	0.016	0.012
Currently married	0.0820	1.943	0.0278	1.276	0.381	0.584
Never married	0.0663	1.595	0.0230	0.826	0.343	0.141
AFQT percentile score	0.0024	2.641	0.0035	8.266	26.529	46.298
Adj. R-square	0.1751		0.2905			
Mean, log hourly wage rate	1.7375		2.0878			
Sample size	742		2.807			

Table 3.14 Determinants of Log Hourly Wage Rate, Regression Results for NLSY Women with Children

Independent variables	All women with children (1)		(2)		Variable means
	Coefficient	T-statistic	Coefficient	T-statistic	
Intercept	1.3863	9.622	1.3479	9.126	1.000
Number of children	-0.0597	-4.895	-0.0059	-0.501	1.895
Age, 1990	0.0265	5.603	0.0023	0.481	29.425
Black	0.0207	0.776	0.648	2.255	0.288
Hispanic	0.0418	1.347	0.1362	4.505	0.159
South	-0.1397	-6.186	-0.1262	-6.005	0.429
Urban and SMSA	0.1011	4.257	0.0708	3.235	0.667
Unemployment rate (local labor market)	-0.0140	-2.315	-0.0121	-2.160	5.718
Ever on welfare	-0.2400	-9.950	-0.0671	-2.615	0.320
Schooling					
0-8 (omitted)					
9-11			-0.0645	-1.106	0.109
12			-0.0102	-0.191	0.501
13-15			0.0831	1.441	0.232

(continued)

Table 3.14 (continued)

| Independent variables | All women with children | | | | | |
| | (1) | | (2) | | Variable means |
	Coefficient	T-statistic	Coefficient	T-statistic	
16+			0.2638	4.093	0.122
Weeks worked					
1986-90			0.0015	9.576	185.100
1980-85			0.0002	1.801	166.698
Worked full time			0.0898	4.037	0.725
Ever armed forces			0.0792	0.982	0.015
Currently married			0.0421	1.294	0.653
Never married			0.0428	1.239	0.208
AFQT percentile score			0.0029	5.470	37.600
Adj. R-square	0.1089		0.2532		
Mean, log hourly wage rate	1.9165		1.9165		
Sample size	2,192		2,192		

the years 1986 through 1990 and 54 percent as many weeks in the preceding period, 1980 through 1985.

- The payoff to additional schooling, particularly for schooling beyond high school is similar for women who have been on welfare and women who have never been on welfare. The return to higher AFQT scores is large and highly significant for both the welfare and nonwelfare groups, but the effect is larger for those who were never on welfare.
- The payoff to additional weeks worked in the 1986-1990 period is large and significant for both groups, although somewhat greater for those never on welfare. Additional work experience in the 1980-1985 period had no impact on later wages for women who had been on welfare, although it had a positive and significant effect (but smaller than for the later period) among those never on welfare.
- When all women are combined in a single analysis, the net effect of having been on welfare can be measured using a variable indicating welfare status. As shown in table 3.14, when we control for no personal characteristics other than age, race and number of children, women ever on welfare are found to earn approximately 24 percent less than women who were never on welfare. After controlling for the full array of variables including weeks worked over the past few years, schooling, and AFQT score, the pay differential is sharply reduced to around 7 percent.

These results are encouraging in some ways, since they suggest that women with a welfare background who acquire skills and work experience and are motivated to work can expect to get a significant payoff in the market as a result of their efforts. Yet the gap in skills related to years of schooling and academic achievement (as measured by AFQT scores) may be extremely difficult to close. Moreover, the factors responsible for welfare in the first place may not be easily reversed.

NOTES

1. The number of AFDC recipients appears to be underreported in the CPS, although the pattern of receipt by age and other characteristics appears to be very similar to that shown in other data sources. See appendix A for further discussion.

2. Since the table uses data from the NLSY, it is limited to women ages 14-22 in 1979. Moreover, the observed durations are limited by the number of years covered by the survey, which at present includes a potential maximum of fourteen years of welfare use.

3. The AFQT has a long history as a reliable indicator of skills and has been used by the Armed Forces for years to determine eligibility for service.

4. Because the test was administered at the same point in time for all NLSY respondents, the scores vary because of differences in age. The scores shown have been statistically adjusted for age variation.

5. The poverty line used for this calculation is the average of the poverty lines for a two-child family of three and a two-child family of four, since about half of the former recipients were married in 1989. Note that the NLSY definition of income includes the reported cash value of food stamps received. However, food stamps were a minor portion of this group's income, adding an average of only $170 to total income for the year.

6. The difference between recent entrants and long-term recipients is larger at younger ages. See appendix table B.1 for 1987 results when the cohort was ages 22-29. In that year, for example, the mean AFQT score of those with two years or less on AFDC was 10 percentage points higher than for those with longer-term participation.

CHAPTER 4

The Effectiveness of Education, Work, and Training Programs for Reducing Welfare Dependence

The idea that education, work, and training programs could be used to improve the employability of welfare recipients has guided government efforts to move recipients off the welfare rolls since at least 1965, when President Lyndon B. Johnson wrote:

> Many recipients of public assistance are capable of training which would ultimately make them self-supporting. I therefore urge the Congress to make permanent the Unemployed Parent and Community Work and Training Programs associated with the Aid to Families with Dependent Children (AFDC) and to require states receiving federal support under AFDC to cooperate in making Community Work and Training available for the unemployed parents of dependent children. (*Economic Report of the President* 1967).

In 1988, Congress reiterated these beliefs when it passed the Family Support Act, which created the Job Opportunities and Basic Skills (JOBS) training program. As explained by a General Accounting Office (GAO) report:

> The (JOBS) program is intended to transform the nation's welfare system b re-focusing the role it plays in helping families in poverty. JOBS requires states to provide parents and teens receiving aid to families with dependent children (AFDC) the education, training, work experience and supportive services they need to move toward self-sufficiency and help avoid long-term welfare dependence. JOBS embodies a new consensus that the well-being of children depends not only on meeting their material needs but

also on the parents' ability to become economically self-sufficient (GAO 1991).

It is clear from these two quotes, over 20 years apart, that the policy community has held to the belief that welfare recipients and their families can be made self-supporting if they are provided with appropriate education, work, and training programs. But what has been the actual impact of these programs on the work effort of participants and on the size of the AFDC caseload? The preceding chapter showed that a significant fraction of AFDC mothers eventually leave the program. Therefore, the question needing to be addressed concerns the extent to which government programs have made a contribution to the outflow that would not have occurred in their absence. Based on the review in this chapter, the overall conclusion we reach is that these programs have had minimal effects on welfare participation over time. The observed flows off the AFDC program among participants in employment and training programs do not appear to have been significantly greater than for similar AFDC mothers who did not participate in such programs.

This section provides an evaluative survey of the major employment and training programs that have been applied to welfare recipients over the past twenty-five years. An important caveat in interpreting the results of this review is that all past programs took place in an environment in which there was no limit on the time an otherwise eligible family could remain on welfare. In recent years, many AFDC recipients have been required to participate in programs and were frequently subject to the sanction of temporary partial benefit loss if they did not comply. However, if a welfare recipient completed a program and then was unable to become self-supporting, she could remain on welfare indefinitely. Faced with a time limit, a recipient might well become more motivated to succeed and therefore utilize her training and employment opportunities more effectively than would have been the case without a time limit. Our finding that the program did not enhance the recipients' earnings rates or upgrade their occupations may have been due partly to lack of motivation by the recipient. Thus, our negative conclusions about the effectiveness of past programs may not necessarily apply to a situation where welfare recipients are faced with a mandatory time limit.

For purposes of this review, we group all education, work, and training programs into three categories: (1) education and training services aimed primarily at more mature women with school-age children; (2) programs of education and special services designed especially for teenage mothers who have recently entered AFDC; and (3) mandatory "workfare" or work-experience programs. The first two categories contain programs that, for the most part, attempted to raise the labor market productivity of the AFDC participant through education, training, and other supportive services. Programs in the third category operated on two levels. First, they may have reduced the caseload by making welfare less attractive, since the recipient was required to devote a significant portion of time to working at a specified location with no increase in benefits. Second, they may have had positive effects on the recipient's productivity in a manner similar to the programs in the first two categories.

Education, Work, and Training Programs for Post-Teenage Mothers

Following smaller efforts in the early 1960s, the Work Incentive (WIN) program, established in 1967 became the first large-scale employment and training program for AFDC recipients. When welfare caseloads continued to rise, more stringent participation requirements were added, and immediate job placement took precedence over training for jobs (WIN II). At its height in 1975, WIN costs totaled about $314 million, which is close to $900 million in today's dollars. But as the high hopes for the program went unfulfilled, WIN funding was not increased in line with inflation during the late 1970s.

An important change was made in the program under the Omnibus Budget Reconciliation Act of 1981 (OBRA). This act authorized states to conduct their own WIN demonstration projects as an alternative to the standard WIN program. Community Work Experience Programs (CWEP) were established, and many states tightened their work requirements. Experience with these OBRA demonstration projects led to the passage of legislation to establish the Family Support Act (FSA) of 1988. The JOBS program, authorized by FSA and required to be implemented in all states by 1990, replaced WIN and stressed both remedial and basic education, as well as training in job skills. JOBS became the framework for providing training services to AFDC recipients. Over the years, many program evaluations using various methodologies have been conducted. One review of the many OBRA demonstration projects evaluated by the Manpower Demonstration Research Corporation (MDRC) concluded as follows:[1]

> The major finding of the MDRC studies is that welfare-to-work programs usually produce the desired type of effects. In most demonstrations, earnings and employment increased; frequently, but not as dependably, welfare payments and welfare participation declined. Typically, the magnitudes of these effects were quite small, particularly regarding welfare receipt (O'Neill 1993).

We come to a similar conclusion after examining the evaluations of four more recent employment and training demonstration projects started under OBRA in the mid- and late 1980s. Table 4.1 provides a description of the four programs—their sites, dates, and basic features. Three of the projects—the Saturation Work Initiative Model (SWIM) in San Diego, the Great Avenues for Independence Program (GAIN) in six California counties, and Project Independence (PI) in nine Florida counties—were mandatory for AFDC recipients with school-age children, with monetary sanctions applied for nonparticipation. The fourth project—The Family Independence Plan (FIP) established in 15 counties in Washington State—provided approximately the same range of education, work, and training services as SWIM, GAIN, and Project Independence. It differed from them in two significant ways, however: (1) special monetary work incentives were built into the program, and (2) no sanctions were applied for nonparticipation.

In the FIP program, participants assigned to an experimental group received cash bonuses for enrolling in the services offered, such as remedial schooling and/or a training program, and an even larger cash bonus was provided if they took a paid job. Consequently, a FIP participant could work and receive, in earnings plus the FIP cash bonus, an amount that would have disqualified her from welfare benefits under the standard AFDC rules. FIP utilized increased marginal work incentives, an approach that had been removed from the AFDC program by the 1981 OBRA Amendments noted above (see O'Neill 1993).

Table 4.1 Features of Four Recent Education-Training Programs

Name	Location	When program started	Period of follow-up evaluation	Mandatory participation and sanctions	Services provided
Saturation Work Incentive Model (SWIM)	San Diego	July 1985	1985 to 1991	Yes	Job search, basic education, training
Greater Avenues for Independence (GAIN)	6 counties in California, including Los Angeles	1985	1989 to 1992	Yes	Job search, basic education, training
Projected Independence (PI)	9 counties in Florida, including Miami	1987	August 1991 to July 1992	Yes	Job search, basic education, training, JOB Club
Family Independence Plan (FIP)	15 counties in Washington State	1988	June 1990 to June 1992	No (positive financial incentive to participate)	Education and training

Two evaluations of the net impacts of FIP (Leigh 1993; Long and Wissoker 1992) found that the program had the perverse effect of actually *increasing* the welfare caseload. Two and three years after FIP started in 1988, the rate of participation in AFDC was much higher among FIP participants than among similar AFDC recipients who had not participated in FIP. The AFDC mothers who did not participate in FIP received no cash bonus for working, and their earnings were subject to the official AFDC rules, which only allowed deductions for certain work expenses and a time-limited income disregard (see above) before reducing benefit amounts dollar for dollar. Thus, it appears that incentives may increase rather than decrease welfare caseloads. (See the discussion in chapter 2 and the analysis in chapter 5).

Unlike FIP, the SWIM and GAIN programs did not utilize earnings disregards, and they provided for monetary sanctions (reduced AFDC monthly benefit amounts) if an eligible recipient refused to participate. SWIM provided job-search training for two weeks, followed by three months in a work-experience program if no job was found during job search. Those still unemployed after completing their work-experience segment were assessed and referred to community education and training programs. GAIN provided for initial testing and screening to find those who might benefit from basic and remedial education. Those who did not need basic education started in job-search training activities and then proceeded through a cycle similar to the SWIM program.

SWIM and GAIN have undergone evaluations conducted by the Manpower Demonstration Research Corporation (MDRC). The MDRC evaluations utilized the methodology of a controlled experiment in which individual recipients were assigned randomly to experimental and control groups (Friedlander, Riccio, and Freedman 1993; Friedlander and Hamilton 1993). MDRC reported that GAIN and SWIM had positive impacts, similar in magnitude to those found for earlier programs operated under WIN and the early OBRA demonstrations.

These positive impacts included modest increases in annual earnings and modest reductions in AFDC benefit amounts, along with smaller effects on rates of program participation. The increases in annual earnings, however, (measured by the observed difference between experimentals and controls) were almost entirely due to increases in the amount of time worked during the year. No significant

differences were found in earnings *rates* per quarter between experimentals and controls in either SWIM or GAIN. Thus, the programs
were unlikely to have had any impact on the long-term earnings capacity of the AFDC recipients who participated. This finding helps explain
why only very small effects were found with respect to welfare participation. Larger reductions in program participation would have required
substantial impacts on the earnings rates, and probably on the occupations, of the participants.

Tables 4.2 and 4.3 present information on the annual earnings and
quarterly earnings of experimentals and controls for the SWIM and
GAIN projects, as reported by the MDRC. It is clear from the tables
that in most comparisons the impact of either SWIM or GAIN on earnings rates (i.e. earnings per quarter of employment) were very small.
(In SWIM the effect on annual earnings declined sharply over time,
and the effect on earnings rates was as often negative as it was positive.) Even the very large percentage increase in annual earnings in the
Riverside GAIN project was almost entirely due to increases in the
amount of time worked per year by the experimentals. The effects of
GAIN, it should be noted, varied widely among the six sites; in Los
Angeles and Tulare no positive impacts could be claimed.

Tables 4.4 and 4.5 present data comparing experimentals and controls with respect to rates of participation in AFDC. While SWIM and
GAIN appear to have reduced welfare participation, the effect was not
very large and appears to have narrowed with time in the program. If
we average over all the comparisons for all the quarters shown in
Tables 4.4 and 4.5, we get a reduction of approximately 4 percentage
points. This is the amount by which the AFDC participation rate of
experimentals was less than that of the controls, on average. However,
by the last quarter shown, this effect was much diminished.

The Project Independence (PI) program was started in Florida in
1987 as its statewide welfare-to-work program. In 1988, after passage
of the Family Security Act, it became Florida's official JOBS program.
Like SWIM and GAIN, participation in PI was mandatory, with sanctions used to punish noncooperative behavior. Also like SWIM and
GAIN, PI provided job-search, occupational training, and basic education components. Each participant was assessed and either assigned
directly to job-search, or first to basic education or training and then to

Table 4.2 Average Annual Earnings and Average Earnings per Quarter Employed for Experimentals and Controls by Follow-Up Period, Single-Parent Family Heads Only (SWIM Program)

Follow-up period	Experimentals	Controls	Percent difference
Average annual earnings[a]			
Quarter[b]			
2 - 5	$2,029	$1,678	21.0
6 - 9	2,892	2,248	28.6
10 - 13	3,287	2,732	20.3
14 - 17	3,775	3,397	11.1
13 - 21	4,126	3,987	3.7
Average earnings per quarter employed			
2 - 5	$1,536	$1,629	(-5.8)
6 - 9	2,056	2,012	2.2
10 - 13	2,391	2,424	(-2.2)
14 - 17	2,816	2,712	3.9
18 - 21	3,100	3,108	(-0.3)

SOURCE: Friedlander and Hamilton 1993.

a. All averages combine the earnings of those who worked with zeros for those who did not work. If the average earnings per quarter are multiplied by four they equal what the average person who did work would have earned if he had worked a full year.

b. Quarters after the random assignment month.

Table 4.3 Average Annual Earnings and Average Earnings per Quarter
Employed for Experimentals and Controls by Follow-Up
Period, Single-Parent Family Heads (GAIN Program by
County Location)

Follow-up period and county	Experimentals	Controls	Percent difference
Alameda	**Average annual earnings**		
Year 1	$1,421	$1,212	17.2
Year 2	2,132	1,609	32.5
	Average earnings per quarter employed		
Year 1	$1,894	$1,782	6.2
Year 2	2,479	2,265	9.4
Butte		Average annual earnings	
Year 1	$2,001	$1,729	15.7
Year 2	2,996	2,442	22.6
	Average earnings per quarter employed		
Year 1	$1,924	$1,746	10.1
Year 2	2,390	2,220	7.6
Los Angeles	**Average annual earnings**		
Year 1	$1,304	$1,308	(-)0.1
Year 2	1,694	1,582	7.0
	Average earnings per quarter employed		
Year 1	$1,889	$2,404	(-)22.5
Year 2	2,258	2,361	(-)4.4
Riverside	**Average annual earnings**		
Year 1	$2,470	$2,550	59.3
Year 2	3,414	2,234	52.8
	Average earnings per quarter employed		
Year 1	$843	$1,845	(-)0.2
Year 2	1,404	2,303	4.4

(continued)

Table 4.3 (continued)

Follow-up period and county	Experimentals	Controls	Percent difference
San Diego	**Average annual earnings**		
Year 1	$2,462	$2,113	16.5
Year 2	3,503	2,794	25.4
	Average earnings per quarter employed		
Year 1	$2,081	$2,031	(-)0.7
Year 2	2,654	2,494	6.4
Tulare	**Average annual earnings**		
Year 1	$1,792	$1,941	(-)7.7
Year 2	2,532	2,498	1.4
	Average earnings per quarter employed		
Year 1	$1,792	$1,866	(-)4.0
Year 2	2,220	2,210	0.4

SOURCE: Friedlander, Riccio, and Freedman 1993.

Table 4.4 AFDC Participation by Follow-Up Period for Experimentals and Controls, Single-Parent Families (SWIM Project)

	Percent not receiving AFDC Benefits	
Follow-up period[a]	Experimentals	Controls
Quarter		
2 - 5	23.7	19.9
6 - 9	44.2	36.9
10 - 13	54.0	48.1
14 - 17	61.2	57.5
18 - 21	65.9	63.9

SOURCE: Friedlander and Hamilton 1993.
a. Quarters after random assignment to program.

Table 4.5 Receipt Status, by Follow-Up Period, for Experimentals and Controls, Single-Parent Families, GAIN Project by County Location (percent still on AFDC)

Follow-up period[a]	Alameda Exp.	Alameda Cont.	Butte Exp.	Butte Cont.	Los Angeles Exp.	Los Angeles Cont.	Riverside Exp.	Riverside Cont.	San Diego Exp.	San Diego Cont.	Tulare Exp.	Tulare Cont.
Quarter												
2	97.0	98.0	88.6	89.4	95.7	95.5	89.4	89.2	94.1	94.7	94.3	93.6
3	94.1	94.8	79.8	76.4	91.8	94.6	75.8	79.6	83.3	85.6	87.0	86.7
4	89.8	91.3	70.7	70.6	88.9	91.6	66.1	72.6	74.8	77.9	81.0	81.0
5	86.0	89.2	65.0	68.4	84.8	88.0	58.7	65.9	69.1	72.1	76.7	75.0
6	83.3	86.8	60.8	63.8	81.8	85.7	54.7	61.1	63.9	67.5	72.3	71.6
7	82.3	83.5	56.2	56.7	79.0	82.5	51.8	57.0	60.3	65.7	68.5	68.7
8	78.8	79.9	51.9	52.7	76.8	79.5	49.1	55.1	58.3	63.7	66.2	64.4
9	76.6	77.1	49.4	47.4	74.0	76.3	46.7	52.0	56.0	61.1	65.4	62.2
10			46.8	48.6	71.5	74.1	45.0	50.4	53.8	58.0		
11			43.2	45.3	69.6	71.2	43.1	49.5	52.2	55.6		
12									50.4	53.9		

SOURCE: Friedlander, Riccio, and Freedman 1993.
a. Quarters after random assignment to program.

job-search. During the 1990-1991 period, the average participation in PI was eight months.

PI underwent a comprehensive evaluation by MDRC (Kemple and Haimson 1994). Table 4.6 summarizes the main findings on program impacts one year after recipients were randomly assigned to the program. The results are very similar to those found in GAIN and SWIM at the same follow-up point—that is, some positive effects that are nonetheless small and may be found to be transitory. If the general magnitude of the caseload effect shown for the GAIN, SWIM, and PI programs is taken at face value, the reduction in the AFDC caseload implied by an effect of this magnitude is about 3 percent if *all* AFDC recipients are put through the program.

Table 4.6 First Year Impacts on Average Earnings of Those Who Worked and AFDC Participation (Project Independence)

Outcome and follow-up period	Program group	Control Group	Percentage difference
Average earnings ($)			
Quarter 2	507	484	4.7
3	642	579	10.9
4	678	648	4.6
5	713	673	5.9
Average earnings of those who worked			
Quarter 2	1,389	1,432	(-)3.1
3	1,725	1,668	3.4
4	1,852	1,857	(-)10.3
5	1,953	1,962	(-)10.5
AFDC participation (percent			
Quarter 2	79.6	81.7	2.6
3	72.2	76.3	5.4
4	66.7	71.6	6.8
5	64.3	68.6	6.3

SOURCE: Kemple and Haimson 1994.

However, this calculation assumes that all AFDC mothers could benefit from a SWIM-, GAIN-, or PI-type program in the same way as AFDC mothers in the experimental groups, which is very unlikely. Moreover, as we discuss below, the impact evaluation methodology used by MDRC assigns credit to the program's services for any case-load-reducing effect that is due solely to the mandatory aspect of the program.[2] Thus, if a recipient who is working "off the books" leaves AFDC when she is mandated to participate in the training program, she would be counted by MDRC as benefiting from the program's services. This practice may overstate the effect of the program services them-selves in reducing welfare participation. To the extent that some por-tion of the observed caseload reduction is due to this "mandatory assignment" effect, it would mean that education and training services by themselves had less impact on aggregate caseload reductions, although the exact amount of impact cannot be discerned from the evaluations conducted.

In sum, the provision of employment and training programs, even in their most recent manifestations (FIP, SWIM, GAIN, and PI), appears to have had only a small impact on reductions in welfare dependence. Whether these programs would be more effective if combined with a two-year limit is an open question.

Education and Other Services Especially for Teenage Mothers

Our longitudinal analysis (chapter 3) indicated that teenagers who bear a child out-of- wedlock have a very high probability of going on welfare and of becoming long-term welfare recipients. Therefore, interest is particularly high in focusing services on this group of wel-fare mothers. They were one of three special target groups identified by Congress in the JOBS program legislation.[3]

Most of the programs designed for teenage welfare mothers have aimed to get dropouts back to school (or to help those who did not drop out to stay in school) with the hope that they would eventually graduate with a high school diploma or GED. The individual recipient was typi-cally assigned to a case manager, whose job was to help the young girl succeed in fulfilling the goals of the program. In addition to high school graduation, these goals usually included birth control counseling, instruction in the care of her child, personal skills development, and introduction to the world of work. Usually local public facilities were utilized for these additional service elements.

Programs of this type have been provided as large demonstration projects under WIN and OBRA, as well as parts of ongoing social welfare programs mainly funded by state and local governments. For example, in New York State a caseworker program has tried to reach all teenagers who gave birth and registered with the AFDC program, either as "case heads" or as dependent teen parents.

Two important programs started in the early and mid-1980s— Project Redirection and the Teenage Parent Demonstration Project— have been the subject of evaluation studies that measure program impacts several years after participants have left the program. Other important programs aimed at young AFDC mothers have been Ohio's Learning, Earning and Parenting Program (LEAP) and the New Chance program evaluated by MDRC (see table 4.7). The LEAP and New Chance programs are more recent and have not yet been subject to comprehensive postprogram outcome evaluations.

Project Redirection

This project was begun in 1980 under the auspices of the Ford Foundation and the WIN program. It operated from 1980 through 1982 and served about 800 teen mothers at four program sites in Boston, New York City, Phoenix, and Riverside, California. About 72 percent of the participating mothers were receiving AFDC benefits when they began the program, and the average participant stayed in the program for about one year. A nonexperimental comparison group was selected by sampling poor teenage mothers in other similar locales with approximately the same set of personal characteristic as the girls in the Project Redirection program. The MDRC analysis shows that the comparison group of girls did receive some services that were similar to those offered by Project Redirection, but not in the same quantities (Polit, Quint and Riccio 1988).

Impact surveys were conducted two years and five years after participants had begun the Project Redirection program; members of the comparison group were also followed-up over the same time period.

Table 4.7 Special Programs for Teenage Mothers in AFDC

Program	Location	Time period of program	Time period of follow-up	Mandatory participation and sanctions	Services provided
Project Redirection	Four sites: Boston, NYC, Phoenix, and Riverside, CA	1980 - 1982	1982 - 1985	No	Case manager, secondary education. special classes in birth control, child care, life problems, etc.
Teenage Parent Demonstration Project (TPDP)	Camden and Newark, NJ and Chicago	1987 - 1991	1989 - 1993	Yes	Case manager, secondary education. Workshops in personal skills, child support, family planning, health and nutrition, life skills, etc.
Learning, Earning and Parenting Program (LEAP)	Ohio (statewide)	1989 - on-going	1980 - 1994	Yes	Case manager, secondary education
New Chance	Nationwide Selected cities: 16 locations in 10 states	1989 - 1991	1991 - 1993	No	Case manager, secondary education. Health-related services, services to benefit children of teen mothers, employment-related services.

Since the average length of stay in Project Redirection was one year, follow-up information was generally gathered from one to four years after program termination.

Four main outcomes are reported for both the Project Redirection participants and the comparison group: educational attainment, employment, welfare dependence, and subsequent pregnancies and live births. With respect to educational attainment and employment, no significant differences were found between participants and the comparison group. The results for welfare dependence were puzzling. At the two-year follow-up point, Project Redirection participants had an AFDC participation rate 7 percentage points above that of comparison group members (75 percent vs. 68 percent). But at the five-year point, the difference reversed and Project Redirection participants showed a lower rate of participation than the comparison group—49 percent vs. 59 percent. Finally, with regard to subsequent fertility, the five-year follow-up reveals the same mean number of subsequent pregnancies (about 3) for both groups, but more abortions were reported for the comparison group. Thus, the Project Redirection group had more live births over the four-year postprogram follow-up period than the comparison group members.

Teenage Parent Demonstration Project (TPDP)

TPDP was evaluated by Mathematica Policy Research, Inc. (Maynard 1993). The TPDP was a large demonstration project operated at three sites—Camden and Newark in New Jersey, and Chicago, Illinois—from late 1987 to mid-1991.

During this period, about 6,000 teenage mothers joined the welfare rolls, and about 90 percent of them were chosen to participate in the experiment. They were randomly assigned to be in the demonstration program or in a control group that only received regular AFDC program services. Unlike Project Redirection, which paid participants a $30 a month bonus just for participating, TPDP had negative sanctions in the form of reduced AFDC payment if they refused to participate in the program altogether, or if they did not keep up with their assigned activities after enrolling (e.g., school attendance).

The cornerstone of TPDP, like Project Redirection, was the provision of multiple services and the use of individual case management. As explained by the Mathematica evaluators:

> Case managers helped participants decide what education or training to pursue, found open slots in appropriate programs, coaxed and pressured the young mothers to stick to their plans, and counseled them when crises arose. If the teenage parents persistently failed to participate in planned activities, case managers initiated sanctions, consisting of reductions in AFDC grants by the amount normally allocated to cover the needs of the mother—generally $160 in New Jersey and $166 in Chicago—which remained effective until the young mothers complied with the participation requirements.
>
> All three demonstration programs required participants to attend a set of initial workshops designed to enhance their personal skills, convey information that would help them cope with their new responsibilities, and prepare them for education, training, and employment activities. Workshop topics included child support, family planning, health and nutrition, life skills, family management, motivation, parenting, employment preparation, education preparation, and HIV and drug abuse prevention.
>
> To help participants move toward self-sufficiency, the demonstration programs promoted participation in education, job training, and/or employment, relying heavily on existing community services. However, they also developed some in-house services, using both their own staff and staff from other agencies. All three programs offered child care and transportation assistance to address these barriers to program participation (Maynard 1993, pp. 5 and 7).

The outcomes of TPDP that are available at this time refer to a period that averages 28 months after program intake for all participants. Participation in TPDP was open-ended—as long as the teenage mother remained on AFDC. One program outcome measured was the rate at which participants left AFDC. Table 4.8 compares the experimentals and controls on this outcome. The results are similar to what was observed in the GAIN and SWIM program evaluations—a definite lowering of participation, but by only a small amount.

Table 4.8 Outcomes of TPDP for Experimentals and Controls by Site of Project

| Site | Percent participating in AFDC | | Average number of pregnancies and live births per participant | | | |
| | | | Pregnancies | | Live births | |
	Experimentals	Control	Experimentals	Control	Experimentals	Control
Camden	78.1	79.8	0.9	1.0	0.6	0.6
Newark	84.4	85.5	1.0	0.9	0.4	0.4
Chicago	75.5	79.2	1.0	1.0	0.8	0.7

SOURCE: Maynard 1993.

Another important outcome measure is fertility behavior. The outcome for TPDP was the same as for Project Redirection. Table 4.8 contains the measures on this outcome for experimentals and controls. The results show both a slightly greater number of pregnancies and live births among experimentals than among controls.

LEAP and New Chance Programs

Some results from Ohio's Learning, Earning, and Parenting Program have been presented in an interim MDRC follow-up evaluation (Bloom, Fellerath, Long, and Woods 1993). Preliminary results have been made available from a small and informal follow-up of 50 participants in the New Chance program (Quint, Fink, and Rowser 1993; Quint, Musick, and Ladner 1994). The results from these two preliminary examinations are not as reliable as MDRC's comprehensive experimental evaluations, but they are suggestive of what the comprehensive follow-up is likely to find.

Each of these programs is similar to one of the two programs for teen mothers described above. New Chance is very similar in spirit and approach to Project Redirection. Participation was voluntary in both programs (i.e., no sanctions were used either to compel initial participation or to continue participation), and positive reenforcement incentives (e.g., better grades in high school led to accumulation of "stamps" that could be traded in for clothing, toys, movies, etc.) were used in both programs as part of a protective and caring environment for the young mothers. In addition, both programs stressed the role of a case manager as a caring adult advisor. Finally, both programs provided significant services and treatments in addition to requirements for high school attendance.

Ohio's LEAP program is similar to the TPDP in that the program participation of young AFDC mothers was mandatory, and penalties were imposed for unsatisfactory participation. On the other hand, LEAP differed from TPDP in that the only major service component was an education program requiring that participants attend high school until a degree was obtained. Employment-related training or courses in health and personal development were not a part of LEAP.

LEAP used quite large monetary incentives, both positive and negative, to keep the young mothers attending school. Each LEAP participart received a bonus of $62 for enrolling in school on time. For each subsequent month that she satisfied the program's attendance requirements, she received an additional $62 per month. The average teen mother in the AFDC program in 1990 received a regular monthly AFDC cash benefit of $274, so the monthly bonus of $62 represented an increase of 22 percent over the base level. In contrast, enrolling late for school resulted in a loss of $62, and unsatisfactory attendance in any month *reduced* the monthly welfare payment by $62. Thus, the total difference in monthly benefits between a teen mother who satisfactorily attended school and one who did not was $124 (=$336-$212). This clearly represents a significant pecuniary incentive for teen mothers in the program to satisfy the attendance requirements of LEAP. It is important to note that the attendance requirement in LEAP was *not* related to any measures of performance in school, such as maintaining a particular grade point average. Rather, it was a simple requirement of physical presence.

A short-run follow-up of early enrollees in LEAP shows that they had better attendance records in high school than the control group of teen mothers who did not receive either the LEAP bonus or penalty. This effect was also found in the evaluation of the TPDP program, in which experimentals attended school in more months than did control group members during the follow-up period. Recall that the TPDP also provided for very large pecuniary penalties for nonparticipation of experimentals.

MDRC followed and interviewed fifty girls (out of a total of 1,550 girls who participated in New Chance during 1989-1992). They found thirty-six who had obtained the program's principal short-term objective. a GED certificate, by the time they left the program, while sixteen girls had left without obtaining the GED.[4] On average, the fifty girls interviewed had been out of the New Chance program for about 30 months at the time of the interview.

Of the thirty-four mothers who had obtained a GED in the New Chance program, the study found that twenty-nine (83 percent) had participated in some kind of postsecondary education and training since obtaining their GED, and twenty-two (65 percent) had worked for some time during their base period. However, at the time of the interview, twenty-five of these mothers (73 percent) were still receiving AFDC benefits. Further, among the sixteen mothers who had not obtained a GED, the study found that all of them were either still in the AFDC program or applying to reenter the program at the time of the interview. Finally, MDRC reports the unfortunately familiar and discouraging finding with regard to subsequent pregnancy—of the thirty-four who obtained their GED, nineteen had become pregnant during the period since obtaining their GED and eleven of these pregnancies resulted in live births.[5] The evaluations of the TPDP and Project Redirection Programs both showed that, in spite of gains on some outcome measures, there were no significant differences between experimentals and controls on subsequent pregnancies and only a small reduction in the rate of AFDC participation.

Given the importance of young mothers in any welfare reform, it is important to develop alternative approaches for reducing their welfare dependence. Clearly, the best way for this population to escape welfare dependency is to avoid having an out-of-wedlock birth in the first place. Unfortunately little is known about how government can go about influencing the fertility behavior of young girls. There has been much discussion of sex education and condom distribution as ways of reducing out-of-wedlock birth. It is not at all clear, however, that ignorance about contraceptive devices is a principal cause of teenage childbearing and subsequent welfare dependence.

Little empirical analysis is available about work and training programs that have served teenage girls from the inner-city *before* they had a child. However, a recent evaluation of the JOBSTART demonstration program (Case et al. 1993) provides evidence suggesting that if young disadvantaged girls can be reached before they have a baby, the probability that they will subsequently go on welfare may be significantly reduced.

The JOBSTART demonstration, implemented between 1985 and 1988, was not directly related to teen pregnancy or the AFDC program. Economically disadvantaged school dropouts age 17 to 21 with poor reading skills participated in education and vocational training and received support services and job placement assistance. Participation in JOBSTART was strictly voluntary, and the program was intended to increase the educational attainment and job prospects of the participating youth.

Although the impact of JOBSTART on earnings outcomes was disappointing, the study did find that AFDC recipiency was significantly lower among the female experimentals who were not custodial mothers at the time they entered JOBSTART. For example, four years after entering the program, 39 percent of the noncustodial girls in the control group were in the AFDC program, while only 31 percent of the corresponding experimental group were. Thus, JOBSTART participation reduced welfare participation by almost 10 percentage points. Among girls who were already custodial mothers when they entered JOBSTART, there was no significant difference in AFDC participation rates between experimentals and controls two years after entry into the program (59.3 percent for experimentals vs. 60.5 percent for controls). The issue of prevention is clearly one that requires more attention than it has received thus far.

Workfare

Another approach to reducing welfare dependency, although widely referred to in the media, is probably the least well defined. To many analysts, the term "workfare" applies to any program for reducing welfare dependency that is mandatory for AFDC recipients. Thus, the GAIN, SWIM, and PI programs described above, all of which were mandatory for certain subgroups of AFDC recipients, have sometimes been referred to as workfare programs. Indeed, the newly created federal-state JOBS program is often called in its entirety a workfare program.

Nevertheless, the term workfare has also been applied to a specific kind of program in which welfare recipients were mandated to perform a particular job for a specified number of hours per week in return for welfare benefits. Formal training and education services have not usually been provided in these programs, and the skill demands of the work have usually been modest. Jobs have been located either in local government agencies or nonprofit organizations, and they could be performed by the recipients with a minimum of informal on-the-job training.

One major objective of this approach—call it "pure" workfare—has been to reduce welfare dependency by reducing the real benefits of welfare; and this has been accomplished by assigning a work requirement to the receipt of welfare benefits. Thus, the work requirement was expected both to deter individuals from enrolling in AFDC, as well as to encourage earlier exits than otherwise would be likely to occur.

In addition, proponents of pure workfare argue that this approach has the potential for providing some valuable services to the community as recipients work for their AFDC benefits. Some observers also have commented that the work experience itself could improve recipients' chances of obtaining a better job in either the private or public sector.[6]

What is the role in the current welfare situation for the pure workfare approach? Is there empirical evidence on its effectiveness in reducing welfare dependence? And what subgroups of the welfare population can it most effectively serve?

Workfare has operated most directly and quickly on those welfare recipients who have fairly good earnings' prospects, including single adults covered by local and state welfare programs (ineligible for federal funding). For those recipients, the value of being on welfare drops sharply when they are mandated to participate in workfare. For recipient groups with low outside earnings prospects relative to benefit levels, including teenage mothers, workfare has been much less likely to have an immediate effect on welfare participation. Although workfare has reduced the net benefit from being on AFDC, recipients would earn little if they went off welfare, so they have tended to remain. Nevertheless, it is possible that in the long run, teenage girls would be deterred by a workfare requirement from having an out-of-wedlock birth in the first place, and would be more motivated to stay in school and enhance their potential earnings.

Chart 4.1 illustrates the impact a workfare program would have on the real gain from welfare and how the situation would differ for high-wage and low-wage welfare recipients. That chart provides a standard economic utility analysis of the individual's choice between leisure time ("discretionary time" is perhaps a better term) and money income. The cash benefit amount is OM. Without a pure workfare program, the individual on welfare would receive this benefit without any loss of leisure time, as indicated by Point 1. With a workfare program, the individual could be at Point 2, where she would still receive the benefit of OM but would have to work PQ hours per week, losing that much in leisure time. Point 1 is clearly preferable to Point 2—that is, pure workfare has reduced the attractiveness of welfare.

But will the welfare recipient leave (or not come on) the program with pure workfare in effect? The answer depends in part on the recipient's potential earnings opportunities off welfare. Two leisure income trade-off lines are shown on the chart. That shown for Recipient A is steeper than that shown for Recipient B, indicating a higher potential wage rate for Recipient A. Recipient A has the option of taking the leisure income bundle available on welfare with pure workfare (Point 2). But if she spends the hours required by workfare (PQ) at a private sector job, she can attain a higher money income than OM (Point 3). Thus, she would be likely to leave (or fail to come on) welfare when pure workfare is present.

Chart 4.1 Analysis of the Impact of Workfare on the Incentive to be on Welfare

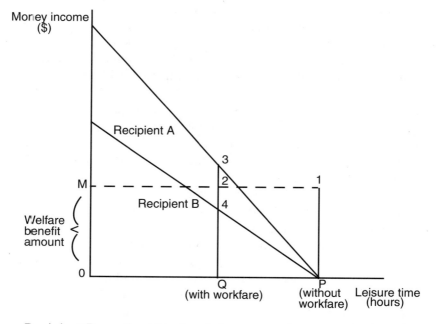

Recipient B, on the other hand, has an earnings capacity less than that of A. Her market earnings from the required PQ hours would put her at Point 4, less than the welfare grant of OM. Consequently, she would not be likely to leave welfare after pure workfare is put in place. A large fraction of welfare recipients are likely to resemble Recipient B.

Little empirical evidence is available concerning the magnitude of the effect of pure workfare on welfare participation. Research has been conducted on one large-scale application of something close to pure workfare conducted in Ohio in the 1980s, and some inferences about workfare can also be drawn from some mandatory educational and training programs.

The Ohio program was evaluated by Schiller and Brasher (1993), who report significant and large impacts of workfare on the AFDC caseload in Ohio. Schiller and Brasher compared AFDC caseloads in Ohio counties that implemented workfare with those that did not. As chart 4.2 shows, the divergence between n experimental and control counties is quite dramatic for the single-parent caseload. Schiller and Brasher applied multiple regression techniques to control for possible factors other than the workfare program that might differ between experimental and control counties. The sizable impact of workfare remained largely intact. The Schiller and Brasher study has been subject of a critical assessment that casts some doubt on the reliability of its findings. Although these criticisms weaken the reliability of the magnitude of the caseload-reducing effect of workfare, they do not appear to negate the finding that a positive and significant effect was present in the Ohio program.[7]

Some additional indirect empirical evidence on the effect of mandatory workfare on welfare caseloads can be obtained from the evaluations of some of the education and training programs discussed above, as well as from some mandatory partial workfare programs that were tried in the early and mid-1980s under OBRA.

Three of the programs discussed above—GAIN, SWIM, and PI— were mandatory for any AFDC recipients who were assigned to them. Thus, for recipients who either had a good job prospect or were working "off-the-books," a mandate to participate in a program like GAIN may have been similar to a mandate to participate in a pure workfare program.[8] One would either lose leisure time or no longer be able to work at an unreported outside job and at the same time collect welfare benefits.

Chart 4.2 Impact Analysis of Ohio's Workplace Program AFDC (Single Parent) Caseload Trends

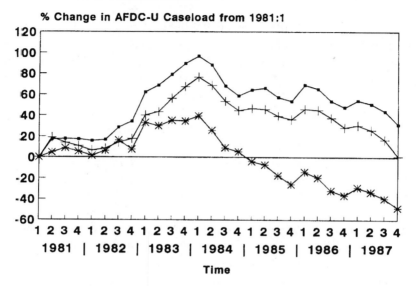

% Change in AFDC-U Caseload from 1981:1

Time

← 60 non-CWEP counties + 20 applicant counties ✳ 8 pilot CWEP counties

SOURCE: Schiller and Brasher 1993, figure 2.

Table 4.9 shows, for those participants in the three recent programs surveyed and two OBRA workfare programs who were assigned to the experimental group, the percent who left the program without receiving any of the services (or performing any of the workfare assignment)

Table 4.9 Percentage of Experimental Group Who Obtained No Services from Their Program

Program	Percent
GAIN	46
SWIM	31
Project Independence	57
San Diego WEP	54
Cook County WEP	52

provided by the program. In each program (except perhaps for SWIM), large percentages of AFDC recipients who were assigned to the experimental group (i.e. those who must show up for program activities) left the program without participating at all. Why would such large proportions leave a mandated program assignment for which they would be sanctioned with reduced benefits? The researchers conducting the evaluation studies made some effort to find out what had happened to these recipients.

The authors of the GAIN study (Friedlander, Riccio, and Freedman 1993) report as follows:

> While a substantial portion of the orientation attenders—ranging from 37 to 57 percent—did not participate in a GAIN activity, almost all of the nonparticipants were people who were not required to participate in GAIN activities by the end of the follow-up period. The vast majority (80 to 100 percent) of the nonparticipants were either no longer enrolled in the program (i.e., they were "deregistered") because they had gotten a full-time job, left welfare, were sanctioned or met other specific criteria, or were temporarily excused from participating because of part-time employment, illness, or other reasons (i.e., they were officially "deferred") (p. 221).

In the PI study (Kemple and Haimson 1994), it is reported that:

> It is not clear how many of those who did not attend orientation left the program because they found a job or because they left the AFDC rolls. In all, However, 70 percent of those who did not attend orientation were employed at some point during the follow-up period, and 66 percent were employed during either the quarter in which they were randomly assigned or the following quarter (p. 60).

If is clear that large numbers of those who immediately left the mandated assignment also left AFDC, the hypothesized effect of workfare on the welfare caseload. However, as the researchers all pointed out, it is not possible to know how much of the exit from AFDC was caused by the mandated assignment and how much reflects ongoing caseload turnover unrelated to the mandated assignment.

In sum, workfare, on both theoretical and empirical grounds, may be capable of reducing welfare caseloads. However, the empirical evidence is scanty and much further research is needed. The recently passed welfare reform bill requires, in effect, a form of workfare for all participants who reach their two-year limits and can no longer receive welfare benefits without spending some time in a work activity (see chapter 1). Should workfare be applied at an earlier point? Mothers whose children are already in school and who are likely to have relatively good job prospects could be a target group for mandatory workfare. Whether or not workfare should be applied to recipients with preschool-aged children before they reach their two-year limit or even at the two-year limit is a more complex question since it involves the potentially large costs of childcare.

Summary

As noted at the beginning of the chapter we feel that our survey indicates that even the most recently conceived education and training programs, and especially those targeted at young teenage mothers, have simply not been effective in raising their earnings capacity, reducing fertility, or reducing the welfare caseload. However, it is possible that combined with a strictly enforced time limit, the education and training programs might have a significant positive effect in reducing welfare caseloads. State welfare administrators should be encouraged to pursue follow-up evaluations of education and training programs operated with the time limit in place.

The general workfare approach (including initiatives that are imbedded in mandatory education and training programs) may be capable of some significant reductions in the welfare caseload, but the empirical evidence is still somewhat thin.

The results for the special programs aimed at teenage AFDC mothers were particularly discouraging and suggest that the emphasis of policy should shift toward the objective of reducing teenage pregnancies.

NOTES

1. Similar findings were reached in evaluations of the traditional WIN programs which preceded the OBRA demonstration projects using statistical evaluation methodologies (Ketron Inc. 1980; Grossman, Maynard, and Roberts 1985).

2. Carol Romero (1994, Appendix A) comes to a similar conclusion about MDRC methodology.

3. In 1993, the GAO found that about 24 percent of teenage mothers on AFDC in 1992 had been served by JOBS, which started in most states in 1990 (GAO 1993).

4. This was not a random sample. Program data show that for all 1,550 New Chance participants, about 24 percent had obtained a GED by the time they left the program.

5. MDRC has released some interim findings on New Chance based on their usual experimental/control group methodology. It reports on girls who had enrolled in the program 18 months before. Their findings are similar to what was reported in the informal follow-up study—no difference in subsequent fertility behavior or welfare participation between experimentals and controls ("New Chance: Interim Findings" Confidential Release, MDRC, June 9, 1994).

6. Based on discussions with Kathy Zall, former director of Employment and Training Programs, Human Resources Administration, New York City. Also Betsy Gotbaum, former commissioner, New York City Parks and Recreation, reported successfully recruiting good employees for regular jobs in her agency from among welfare recipients who had been assigned to the Parks Department under a workfare program mandated by the city for its Home Relief recipients. (Home Relief is a state and locally funded welfare program for single individuals.)

7. The critical assessment alluded to was written by Ralph Smith of the Congressional Budget Office (CBO), who reviewed the Schiller-Brasher study when it first appeared in 1988 (internal memo—copy available on request). Smith's criticism notes that there were only eight experimental counties (vs. 80 nonexperimental counties) and the experimentals may have been subject to special factors not controlled for in the multiple regression analysis. For example, these eight counties may have been trending down in terms of their AFDC caseloads before the experiment began.

8. It is not identical because there is the opportunity of joining an education or training program (some areas offer college education opportunities). If the participant puts some value on these opportunities, she may not leave.

CHAPTER 5

Administrative and Incentive Changes Under the Jobs Program

What Did They Do for Welfare Reform?

In 1988 the JOBS program had been hailed as an approach that would reduce welfare dependency both by providing the education and training services described above and by changing the way welfare programs were administered. Under JOBS, the AFDC program was to have become a vehicle for developing the work motivation and skills of clients, rather than a system for determining eligibility and dispensing checks. Moreover, states were encouraged to experiment with changes in the rules and incentives of their AFDC programs to see if they could reduce welfare dependency. Under the new welfare legislation, states will have the freedom to continue the experiments started under JOBS as well as to develop additional changes in rules and incentives.

Did the JOBS framework actually provide these kinds of changes in the administration of the AFDC program? Has the state waiver program led to experiments that have resulted, or are likely to result, in a reduced welfare caseload? We examine some evidence on each of these questions.[1]

Administrative Objectives Under JOBS

Here we examine two kinds of indirect evidence: types of services provided and recipients served, and overall coverage and utilization of JOBS services by the AFDC population.

Types of Services Provided and Recipients Served

Table 5.1 shows that in FY91 most of the participants in the JOBS program were in a formal education program (elementary, secondary or postsecondary) or in a formal training program. There was little use of any program element resembling workfare, such as Community Work Experiences Programs (CWEP). This is no surprise because the 1988 legislation that established JOBS stipulated that formal education and training activities should be the main focus. Only four states—Colorado, Nevada, Ohio and West Virginia—have placed a significant fraction of their JOBS resources into CWEP. This emphasis on formal education and training constituted a sharp break from the OBRA-WIN program approach that immediately preceded JOBS. Under OBRA-WIN, a greater emphasis was placed on CWEP-type activities.

Table 5.1 Average Monthly Percentage of JOBS Participants Distributed by Service Component, Fiscal Year 1992: U.S. Total

Types of JOBS service	Percent of total enrolled
Education	
High school	29.3
Post secondary	17.8
Vocational training	7.5
Jobs skill training	11.4
Jobs readiness	5.4
Job development and entry	10.3
Job search	11.3
On-the-job training	0.5
Work supplementation	0.1
CWEP	4.4
Other	1.9
Total*	100.0
Total number of participants[a]	403,653

SOURCE: Derived from table 10-6, *1994 Green Book*, U.S. House of Representatives, Committee on Ways and Means.

a. The total excludes those who are listed as in "assessment/employment plan." Each component is shown as a percentage of this adjusted total. Percentages may not add to 100 percent due to rounding.

The JOBS legislation also targets specific subgroups of AFDC recipients—the long-term AFDC recipient and, especially, the teen-age mother who has not received a high school diploma. Yet a recent GAO survey (GAO 1993) estimated that only about 24 percent of all AFDC parents under 20 years of age were being served by JOBS. These young mothers were almost exclusively enrolled in secondary school in either a regular degree program or a GED program. Of the teen mothers served by JOBS, about 25 percent were also receiving some type of special support service for teen mothers such as "life-skills" training or prenatal classes. For these few AFDC teen mothers, the treatment under JOBS was similar to the treatment received under Project Redirection and the Teen Parent Demonstration Project, reviewed earlier.

The remaining JOBS participants were drawn from other targeted groups, such as mothers whose youngest child is within two years of age 18, and from nontargeted groups who are generally short-term AFDC recipients.

Overall Coverage and Utilization of JOBS by States

The 1988 JOBS legislation required that certain percentages of non-exempt AFDC recipients participate in JOBS activities if the state was to continue receiving federal matching funds for JOBS. This requirement generated a management information system under which the states reported each year on the percentage of all AFDC recipients who are nonexempt (i.e., are "mandatory" for participation in JOBS) and the percent of these mandatory participants who did in fact participate. Did JOBS lead to large percentages of AFDC mothers being made mandatory and required to participate in training and other programs? And has JOBS been more effective than previous work and training regimes in inducing participation?

The 1988 law, as well as other programs that preceded JOBS (OBRA-WIN), allowed for exemptions from participation in work-education-training programs. The most important reason for exemption has always been the presence of pre-school-age children, either under age 6 (pre-JOBS) or under age 3 (JOBS). JOBS is more complicated than pre-JOBS programs with regard to the young child exemption, however. Under JOBS, a child between ages 3 and 6 can trigger an exemption if childcare services are not guaranteed to the mother. On the other hand, an AFDC mother who is younger than 20 years of age, is not enrolled in school and does not have a high school diploma must participate in JOBS, regardless of the age of her child. Further, JOBS allows states to reduce the minimum age at which a child qualifies a mother for exemption to 1 year old.

Table 5.2 shows the percentage of AFDC adult recipients who are nonexempt from JOBS, ("mandatories"), the percentage of these AFDC mandatories who were participants in JOBS, and the percent of JOBS participants among all AFDC adult recipients for FY 91, FY 92, and FY 94, by state and for the entire U.S.

On average, across states, 43 percent of the AFDC adult recipients are found to be mandatories for JOBS—meaning that slightly less than 60 percent of AFDC adult recipients were exempt from the program. A 60 percent exemption rate is larger than the fraction of AFDC recipient children who are under 3 years of age (about 25 percent across states) and even larger than the fraction of children under age 6 (about 40 percent). As table 5.3 shows, about 73 percent of all exemptions arise because of the presence of children below the age cut-off. Thus, almost all preschool children on AFDC must have been providing exemptions for their mothers—with other factors, such as having a sick child, providing the remainder of exemptions. Since JOBS does not require mothers to participate when childcare is lacking, this finding may reflect limitations on childcare resources, although it might also reflect a lack of enthusiasm by welfare administrators for enforcing the JOBS participation obligation.

The large variation across states in these percentages probably reflects these same factors—variation in the percent of children under 3 and 6, availability of child care resources, and variable enforcement by welfare administrators.

A comparison of columns 8 and 9 in table 5.2 shows that, although 22 percent of the JOBS mandatories were participating in JOBS activities (in FY 94), these participants account for only 9 percent of all AFDC recipients. Thus, to increase the overall JOBS participation rate (the percent of all welfare recipients in JOBS) to a level of 60 or 70 percent would require a very large increase in resources over current levels—with a large amount needed for child care services

Table 5.2 Percent of AFDC Caseload Mandatory for JOBS, Percent Mandatories Participating in JOBS, and Percent Caseload Participating in JOBS, FY 1991, 1992, 1994

State	(1) FY 1991 % of AFDC adults mandatory for JOBS	(2) FY 1991 % of mandatories participating in JOBS	(3) % of AFDC adults participating in JOBS	(4) % of AFDC adults mandatory for JOBS	(5) FY 1992 % of mandatories participating in JOBS	(6) % of AFDC adults participating in JOBS	(7) % of AFDC adults mandatory for JOBS	(8) FY 1994 % of mandatories participating in JOBS	(9) % of AFDC adults participating in JOBS
U.S. (total)	39	15	6	43	17	7	43	22	9
Alabama	17	26	4	26	30	8	25	62	15
Alaska	27	16	4	22	18	4	27	23	6
Arizona	21	12	3	25	11	3	19	17	3
Arkansas	38	24	9	37	24	9	23	20	5
California	36	14	5	39	12	5	42	19	8
Colorado	69	14	10	70	17	12	71	15	11
Connecticut	52	27	14	61	24	15	56	21	12
Delaware	31	28	9	41	18	7	39	19	7
District of Columbia	37	9	3	51	12	6	48	10	5
Florida	24	19	5	26	15	4	19	31	6
Georgia	32	10	3	39	12	5	42	22	9
Hawaii	6	9	1	7	10	1	37	15	5
Idaho	20	27	5	21	39	8	25	39	10
Illinois	54	11	6	57	11	6	55	20	11
Indiana	18	7	1	39	6	2	40	23	9

Table 5.2 (continued)

State	(1) FY 1991 % of AFDC adults mandatory for JOBS	(2) FY 1991 % of mandatories participating in JOBS	(3) % of AFDC adults participating in JOBS	(4) % of AFDC adults mandatory for JOBS	(5) FY 1992 % of mandatories participating in JOBS	(6) % of AFDC adults participating in JOBS	(7) % of AFDC adults mandatory for JOBS	(8) FY 1994 % of mandatories participating in JOBS	(9) % of AFDC adults participating in JOBS
Iowa	32	10	3	32	12	4	39	16	6
Kansas	54	6	3	56	20	11	59	36	21
Kentucky	18	23	4	24	20	5	59	20	12
Louisiana	24	9	2	33	13	4	40	23	9
Maine	49	7	3	55	9	5	55	23	13
Maryland	50	6	3	50	10	5	40	18	7
Massachusetts	43	39	17	50	32	16	50	17	9
Michigan	57	12	7	56	17	10	64	21	13
Minnesota	46	8	4	29	16	5	35	19	7
Mississippi	12	3	0.4	20	13	3	48	18	9
Missouri	24	8	2	29	14	4	38	17	6
Montana	58	25	15	90	17	15	52	28	14
Nebraska	38	73	28	41	77	32	45	76	34
Nevada	21	16	3	28	15	4	37	17	6
New Hampshire	34	23	8	40	25	10	41	41	17
New Jersey	52	14	7	56	14	8	61	18	11
New Mexico	35	18	6	28	26	7	33	28	9

New York	43	10	4	45	14	6	46	19	9
North Carolina	28	9	3	38	14	5	41	20	8
North Dakota	38	26	10	37	31	11	36	29	10
Ohio	52	15	8	54	19	10	16	29	13
Oklahoma	68	45	31	70	32	22	44	9	4
Oregon	39	20	8	48	21	10	57	30	17
Pennsylvania	45	10	5	46	13	6	49	19	9
Rhode Island	56	17	10	63	14	9	70	16	11
South Carolina	23	20	5	35	16	6	26	29	7
South Dakota	29	25	7	34	25	9	50	57	29
Tennessee	16	11	2	20	20	4	22	24	5
Texas	41	12	5	46	12	6	33	17	6
Utah	67	43	29	84	35	29	69	51	35
Vermont	55	11	6	51	14	7	50	15	7
Virginia	29	16	5	36	18	6	38	19	7
Washington	27	16	4	36	31	11	36	37	13
West Virginia	60	13	8	52	13	7	48	28	13
Wisconsin	52	39	20	53	32	17	41	32	13
Wyoming	33	44	15	34	31	11	52	52	27

SOURCE: U.S. House of Representatives, Committee on Ways and Means, Green Book: FY 1991, 1993 edition (table 7, pp. 642-644), FY 1992, 1994 edition (table 10-8, pp. 357-359, FY 1994, 1996 edition (table 8-9, pp. 425-427).

Table 5.3 AFDC Adult Recipients Exempt from Work Programs by Reason for Exemption

Year	Total exempt adults	Percent distribution				
		Aged, poor health	Child underage	Student	Employed	Other
1987	1,980,604	8.4	72.5	0.5	1.9	16.7
1991	2,327,525	8.7	72.8	1.4	2.9	14.2

SOURCE: Characteristics and Financial Circumstances of AFDC Recipients, FY 1991 and FY 1987 U.S. Department of Health and Human Services, Office of Family Assistance, Washington, DC.

Table 5.4 compares the percentage of AFDC recipients who were mandatory registrants for work and training programs in FY 1986, 1987, and 1992. During 1986 and 1987, the OBRA-WIN program was in force, and in 1992 JOBS was in operation. As noted, under OBRA-WIN any child under age 6 would trigger an exemption, while under JOBS the exemption age could be 3 if childcare were available and could be eliminated entirely if the schooling attained by the AFDC teenage mother were less than a high school degree. In general, since the exemption requirements are more stringent under JOBS, we would expect to find a larger percent subject to the mandate under JOBS than under OBRA-WIN.

The data in table 5.4 show that this is not the case. The mandatory percentages are about the same under the two regimes. And table 5.3 shows that the reasons for being nonmandatory (exempt from work-training programs) were very similar under JOBS and OBRA-WIN. Clearly, the presence of a young, and especially a pre-school-age, child has always been a very important barrier to participation in education and training programs. Moreover, the data in table 5.4 suggest that this problem may be as strong as ever in spite of the pressures to promote employability activities surrounding the JOBS program. However, the small increase in the percent participating in JOBS activities in FY 94 suggests some improvement may have been made under JOBS. Again, we cannot be sure if the low mandatory participation rates reflect lack of child care resources or a resistant attitude by administrators.

Table 5.4 Percent of Adult AFDC Recipients who were Mandatory Registrants for Work and Training Programs, by State, Fiscal Years 1986, 1987, 1992

State	FY 1986	FY 1987	FY 1992
Alabama	23	19	26
Alaska	18	16	22
Arizona	22	23	25
Arkansas	41	55	37
California	30	30	39
Colorado	29	28	70
Connecticut	36	36	61
Delaware	30	29	41
District of Columbia	27	29	51
Florida	23	71	26
Georgia	26	25	39
Hawaii	17	14	7
Idaho	30	30	21
Illinois	32	32	57
Indiana	39	53	39
Iowa	24	26	32
Kansas	24	23	56
Kentucky	24	60	24
Louisiana	15	8	33
Maine	23	26	55
Maryland	31	27	50
Massachusetts	43	47	50
Michigan	91	91	56
Minnesota	23	26	29
Mississippi	10	5	20
Missouri	16	15	29
Montana	27	28	90

(continued)

Table 5.4 (continued)

State	FY 1986	FY 1987	FY 1992
Nebraska	97	97	41
Nevada	18	20	28
New Hampshire	27	25	40
New Jersey	41	41	56
New Mexico	17	19	28
New York	32	30	45
North Carolina	38	37	38
North Dakota	42	41	37
Ohio	32	30	54
Oklahoma	92	93	70
Oregon	40	35	48
Pennsylvania	97	96	46
Rhode Island	33	36	63
South Carolina	22	18	35
South Dakota	35	34	34
Tennessee	46	51	20
Texas	30	39	46
Utah	21	19	84
Vermont	21	44	51
Virginia	36	32	36
Washington	27	28	36
West Virginia	37	40	52
Wisconsin	28	31	53
Wyoming	39	35	34
U.S. Total	39	40	43

SOURCE: Columns (1) and (2) are from *Characteristics and Financial Circumstances of AFDC Recipients*, FY86 and FY87, U.S. Department of Health and Human Services, Office of Family Assistance. Column (3) is from *1994 Green Book*, U.S. House of Representatives, Committee on Ways and Means.

Finally, table 5.5 shows the percentage of female AFDC participants who were employed (either full time or part time) at the end of the fiscal years 1987 and 1991.[2] Again, there is little sign that the impact of JOBS on the employability and work incentives of AFDC recipients is any greater than that of earlier programs with similar goals. However, because economic conditions were less favorable in 1991 than in 1987, it is possible that JOBS has improved utilization of training-employment activities.

Program Experiments by States under the JOBS Waiver Program

Like the OBRA-WIN program before it, the JOBS program has allowed individual states to make experimental modifications and changes in their individual state AFDC programs. Some states appeared quite eager to experiment with program changes in order to improve their overall AFDC programs. By early 1996, 44 states were involved in special experimental changes that required waivers from the federal government.[3]

Our review is in two parts. The first part covers two types of experiments that, although aimed at getting people to leave welfare, may have the unintended effect of providing people with incentives to join the rolls. The experiments in the second group do not have this type of side effect.

Experiments with Marginal Work Incentives and with the AFDC-UP Program

Thirty of the forty-four states operating under program waivers have been experimenting with some form of marginal work incentive provision that is more generous than the provisions contained in the federal rules.[4] In addition, thirty-three states have been experimenting with eliminating the work experience rule for the eligibility of a two-parent family for the AFDC-UP part of the AFDC program.

Table 5.5 Percent of Female AFDC Recipients Who Were Employed (either Part Time or Full Time), Pre-JOBS (1987) and Post-JOBS (1991), by State of Residence

State	June 1987	June 1991
Alabama	4.2	3.0
Alaska	6.3	10.7
Arizona	4.9	5.1
Arkansas	5.6	5.5
California	5.3	6.3
Colorado	8.2	6.0
Connecticut	6.7	5.3
Delaware	5.8	8.7
District of Columbia	4.8	1.8
Florida	7.5	6.1
Georgia	2.5	5.5
Hawaii	5.9	13.8
Idaho	7.0	13.9
Illinois	2.9	4.0
Indiana	10.3	8.5
Iowa	15.8	15.8
Kansas	10.2	12.6
Kentucky	3.7	11.1
Louisiana	0.7	2.6
Maine	7.9	15.2
Maryland	3.3	3.7
Massachusetts	7.4	4.5
Michigan	9.3	11.7
Minnesota	14.4	11.4
Mississippi	4.1	12.1
Missouri	6.5	6.2
Montana	12.3	12.1

State	June 1987	June 1991
Nebraska	15.9	15.6
Nevada	4.7	2.5
New Hampshire	9.5	5.5
New Jersey	2.9	2.5
New Mexico	5.2	7.2
New York	4.0	2.9
North Carolina	3.9	13.0
North Dakota	17.6	16.0
Ohio	3.7	5.2
Oklahoma	6.7	5.8
Oregon	14.0	10.0
Pennsylvania	3.6	2.8
Rhode Island	8.3	3.9
South Carolina	8.2	11.2
South Dakota	15.6	12.4
Tennessee	6.7	9.2
Texas	3.2	4.1
Utah	20.4	20.0
Vermont	11.3	8.9
Virginia	7.6	4.8
Washington	7.9	8.4
West Virginia	4.7	1.9
Wisconsin	15.9	16.1
Wyoming	7.4	26.1
Guam	0.6	2.1
Puerto Rico	0.3	0.1
Virgin Islands	2.5	3.0
U.S. Total	5.8	6.4

SOURCE: *Characteristics and Financial Circumstances of AFDC Recipients, FY 1991 and FY 1987*, U.S. Department of Health and Human Services, Office of Family Assistance, Washington, D.C.

Marginal Work Incentives

In 1995, except for $190 a month that could be deducted for work and childcare expenses and $30 a month that was "disregarded," a working AFDC mother's earnings were all subtracted from her AFDC benefit amount. Moreover, the $30 monthly income disregard was only allowed during the mother's first year on the program. The AFDC amount was then reduced by all of the recipient's remaining net earnings—sometimes called a "100 percent implicit tax on net earnings."

The various experimental disregard programs all increased the amount of net earnings that could be disregarded. For example, in California, the first $30 plus 33 percent of the remaining net earnings have been disregarded, with no time limit on the disregard. In Michigan, the disregard has been $200 a month plus 20 percent of the remaining net earnings.

These disregards were aimed at providing existing welfare recipients with a monetary incentive to work—that is, the recipients could add to their total income by working because their net earnings would not be fully deducted from their AFDC benefit amount. On the other hand, even though these disregards may have increased work effort among AFDC recipients, there is no empirical evidence over the history of their use (1967-1981) and nonuse (1982-present) to suggest that they also got recipients to leave the program entirely. This is not really surprising, given the fact that earnings disregards by themselves do not give a recipient a pecuniary incentive to leave the program. However, the earnings disregards do provide an incentive to work while on welfare and to combine some level of earnings with some reduced benefit amount.

The way these effects are expected to operate is illustrated in chart 5.1. Note that the disregard expands the recipient's potential income for a given number of hours worked while on welfare. Supporters of earnings disregards argue that recipients will be prompted to leave the welfare program as their earnings in the private sector grow due to increased work experience. They claim that the disregard operates by first inducing the recipient to try working while still receiving welfare benefits, and then motivating the recipient to get on-the-job training to raise her earnings capacity to a level that makes leaving welfare attractive financially. This process can move a recipient off the program, but only if the slope of her off-program budget line, which equals her wage rate, as shown in chart 5.1, does in fact pivot (at point L_0) to the right by a significant amount.

Chart 5.1 Analysis of the Effect of Earnings Disregards on the Incentive to Come On and to Leave Welfare

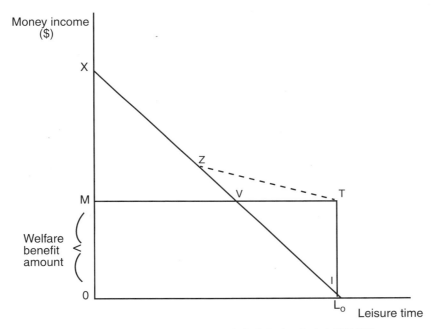

NOTE: Without an earnings disregard the individual's budget line is L_0TVX. With an earnings disregard the budget line becomes L_0TZX.

What proponents of disregards have usually overlooked is that in addition to stimulating work among women on welfare—a good effect—they can also provide a pecuniary incentive for women not on welfare to come into the program. This can also be illustrated in chart 5.1. In the absence of a disregard, the budget line confronting a potential welfare program entrant (L_0TVX) is such that she would not come on the program because she is on her budget line between points V and X. Her earnings rate in the private sector and her preferences between money income and leisure are such that the welfare benefit amount itself (L_0T) is not enough for her to go into the program. However, when a positive disregard rate is introduced to the picture, her budget line on welfare pivots up to (L_0TZX) and she might now enter the program and reduce her hours of work—locating somewhere on the segment TZ. Now the combination of reduced earnings and partial welfare benefits is more attractive than her income off welfare.

There is some empirical evidence on the caseload-increasing effects of earnings disregards.[5] For example, we saw previously that the Family Independence Plan (FIP) program contained a generous earnings disregard for AFDC women in the treatment group and that the evaluation of FIP reported caseload increases. It is not clear how earnings disregards would interact with strict time limits under the new welfare legislature. The strict time limit gives recipients the incentive to become job-ready, and whether they need the extra incentives of the disregard is not obvious. As noted for training programs, state welfare administrators should carefully monitor the possible caseload effects of marginal disregard increases.

AFDC-UP Program

The AFDC-UP Program was an optional program for states up to 1990. After that, it was mandatory for every state to provide a program for families with dependent children in which both parents were present but neither can locate a job. The federal rules limited participation in AFDC-UP to those families in which at least one of the parents had significant work experience in the four years preceding application for AFDC-UP. More specifically, parents had to have worked in six quarters out of the twelve quarters that preceded their time of application for AFDC-UP. This work-experience requirement is similar to that used by the unemployment insurance (UI) program. In addition the AFDC-UP program required that a spouse who goes back to work does not work more than 100 hours a month. Working more than 100 hours, even if earnings are still low enough for eligibility, would lead to loss of eligibility.

The reason for the work-experience requirement was to restrict the benefits of the program to those who have demonstrated a serious attachment to the labor force. The requirement excluded unemployed families who had just entered the labor force until they had demonstrated the requisite attachment by accumulating work experience.

States that have experimented with dropping the work-experience requirement for their AFDC-UP program were hoping that it would keep young couples together who otherwise would split up in order to obtain AFDC benefits. A young couple with a dependent child but no job or work experience could come into the AFDC-UP program as an intact family in those states with this experiment in place (Alabama, Florida, Michigan, Illinois, and Vermont).

A potential problem with this approach was similar to that suggested for the earnings disregard—that is, some young, unemployed married couples who would not have divorced or separated to go on welfare would have an incentive to participate in the AFDC-UP program. Young couples with limited skills and little work experience generally start out with low-paying jobs and may have a hard time finding and deciding among job options. With the work-experience requirement waived, some of them may have been tempted to delay this stressful process by taking advantage of AFDC-UP. The situation is similar for the 100-hour rule. Its purpose was to discourage couples from using AFDC benefits to finance their marriage by sharply limiting the amount of income they could obtain while collecting AFDC-UP benefits. Again, some married couples who would not have split up to collect AFDC benefits with the 100-hour rule would have been tempted to go on AFDC when it was lifted in the experiment.

Other Experiments

Most of the remaining state experiments under the JOBS waiver program fall into three groups: time-limit experiments, experiments that limited the additional benefits that could be obtained when a child is born after the family was on the program, and various rules and sanctions relating to participation in the JOBS education and training program activities. There are other types of experiments with childcare provisions, responsibilities of grandparents and step-parents, and initiatives related to children and teen parents, which we do not comment on.

Two-Year Limits

Thirteen states, including Florida, Iowa, Vermont, and Wisconsin, have set up experiments under which some recipients in some locations in the state were told that they can only collect benefits for a specific and limited period of time.

Florida's experiment was conducted in only two counties in the state. The plan limited recipients to no more than 24 months of AFDC benefits in any 60-month period or more than 36 months of benefits in any 72-month period. The particular time-limit group a recipient was assigned to depended on family characteristics. The plan allowed families who lost AFDC benefits under the experiment to keep their Medicaid eligibility. Moreover, there was no provision requiring a specified minimum time to elapse between the exhaustion of benefit payments and renewed welfare eligibility. Thus, immediately after 60 months or 72 months, the family would be eligible for 24 or 36 more weeks of benefits.

Iowa's plan, which was put in force statewide, did not mention a specific time limit. The plan simply states that "once JOBS participants have reached the end of a mutually agreed upon time frame for achieving self-sufficiency, benefits are terminated (with a possible extension for good cause)."

Vermont's time-limit experiment, also enforced statewide since July 1994, required that after 30 months of AFDC, a family head must obtain his/her own job or participate in subsidized community service employment.

Wisconsin's experiment operated in two counties and was similar to Florida's—i.e., benefits could be collected for up to 24 months within a 48-month period. However, unlike Florida, Wisconsin required a minimum time period of 36 months to elapse between the collection of the last AFDC monthly payment and the receipt of additional AFDC benefits. On the other hand, both the Florida and Wisconsin time-limit experiments allowed recipients to return to welfare after some predetermined period had elapsed.

Additional Children and Benefits

Twenty states have had some form of limit on how much benefits would increase when an AFDC family had an additional child that was conceived while the parents were on welfare. Georgia, New Jersey, and Wisconsin, for example, have had experimental programs that limit the amount of cash AFDC benefits a family could obtain when the family has another child while already on the program. The food stamp allotment did increase for the additional child, however.

Both Georgia and New Jersey allowed no increase in the AFDC cash benefit for an additional child, and both states were explicit in saying that what made the family ineligible for a benefit increase was the conception of the additional child after the family had gone on AFDC. Wisconsin allowed the family one-half of the usual per child cash allowance for the "second child born" and nothing for the third and additional children born. Wisconsin's program statement did not mention whether time of conception or birth governed this determination.

Utilization of JOBS Services

States have experimented with ways to increase the utilization of their JOBS program's educational and training services. One approach has been to extend permission for use of the services to the noncustodial parent of an AFDC child— usually the father. Another has been to specify that only mothers with very young children (e.g., less than six months) can be excused from participating in JOBS activities.

Some states also require AFDC children age 14 or older to participate in JOBS, and some states reserve the right to cut off benefits if recipients, who are mandatory for JOBS, fail to participate.

Summary

Our review suggests that the JOBS legislative-administrative apparatus made, at best, only marginal improvement over past regimes in utilizing work and training programs to reduce the welfare caseload. The AFDC program has been, for all practical purposes, dominated administratively by the individual state welfare administrators. Thus it remains to be seen whether the efforts of the federal government to mandate participation under the new welfare program will produce any results unless the states really believe that education and training will greatly reduce welfare caseloads.

The wide range of experiments launched by the states under the JOBS waiver provisions, however, is a very hopeful sign. It suggests that giving more discretion to the states might lead to innovative approaches to the problem of reducing welfare caseloads and easing the transition to work. However, as noted, it is too early to assess the results of the experiments started in the early 1990s. Since this was a period that included a recession and then a full-scale recovery, it will be difficult to separate out the effects of the waiver experiments on the AFDC caseload from the effects of the changes in the economy.

NOTES

1. The study by Greenberg and Wiseman (1992) presents an interesting analysis of how the OBRA administrative framework influenced the JOBS program.

2. These figures refer to work activities that are reported to the program. There is some evidence that AFDC recipients underreported their earnings.

3. Periodic summaries of state waivers are prepared by the American Public Welfare Association and by the Center for Law and Social Policy (CLASP).

4. The amount of coverage of any waiver program within a state varies from total coverage to coverages of only a small part of the state's AFDC program.

5. See chapters 2 and 4.

CHAPTER 6

Summary and Concluding Comments

In recent years there has been growing concern that the AFDC program has fostered welfare dependency and encouraged the formation of female-headed families. Such concerns have spurred widespread support for legislation that would significantly restrict eligibility for benefits and in other ways reduce the attractiveness of the program. The new law that replaces AFDC makes many such changes, including the imposition of a five-year lifetime limit on receipt of welfare and stiffer work requirements during periods of welfare receipt. Significantly, the law also gives the states substantially more power to determine eligibility, benefit structure, and program provisions than was the case under AFDC.

This study presented data and analysis bearing on three key aspects of welfare participation that the states will have to consider as they determine the best way to implement the new welfare legislation. One is the effect of financial incentives in the welfare benefit system on welfare participation. The second involves the patterns of welfare use and the work skills and other characteristics of short- and long-term welfare recipients. The third is the effectiveness of the many work and training programs for welfare participants that have been tried over the past twenty-five years.

The Effect of Financial Incentives

The new law will reduce the value of going on welfare in several ways. The imposition of a five-year time limit significantly reduces the potential benefit that could be accumulated over a life time. A mandatory work requirement after two years in the program imposes costs on recipients who will lose free time. Block grants could lead states to provide lower benefits than would otherwise be the case.

An important question then is how individuals will respond to the reduced income stream offered by welfare. Will the changed incentives induce current recipients to leave welfare, through work or marriage, sooner than was the case in the old AFDC program? Will the new provisions discourage entry into welfare in the first place and reverse the trend of increasing formation of female-headed families, particularly through out-of-wedlock childbearing? Or will the primary effect of these changes be to increase poverty with little or no change in the work or marital behavior of recipients forced to leave the program, or in the motivation of young women to take steps to avoid welfare dependency?

Research cannot give definitive answers to these questions. However, the analysis in chapter 2 suggests that individuals are responsive to changes in the level of benefits provided by the welfare system. The growth in the welfare caseload since the mid 1960s is consistent with the growth in the value of the total benefit package (including the AFDC cash benefit plus Food Stamps and Medicaid) which was 60 percent higher in 1994, after adjusting for inflation, than the value of benefits in 1964 when benefits were largely confined to the AFDC cash component alone. The benefit-restricting changes incorporated in the Omnibus Budget Reconciliation Act of 1981 (OBRA) also appear to have reduced the caseload. With respect to the effects of welfare on the increase in female-headed families, recent research (cited in chapter 2) suggests that welfare has had a negative effect on marriage and a positive effect on out-of-wedlock childbearing, although the importance of these effects is variable across studies. Because the new legislation will reduce the value of going on welfare, we anticipate that it will induce reduction in the welfare caseload. The impact may be greater in the long run as attitudes of future cohorts of young women may be influenced by the legislation, causing some decline in out-of-wedlock childbearing and increases in marriage and work.

Characteristics of the Welfare Population

The characteristics and behavior patterns of the current welfare population are bound to influence the practical implementation of welfare reform by the states. Given a 5-year time limit it becomes important to know the number who have exceeded the limit under AFDC and to be able to determine, based on skills and other characteristics, which recipients are most likely to encounter problems.

As shown in chapter 3, which analyzes the welfare usage of a national sample of young women followed over a thirteen-year period, there is considerable diversity in recipient behavior. Counting all episodes on welfare over the thirteen years, we find that more than 40 percent of mothers who ever go on welfare eventually accumulate more than five years on the program. But another group seems to stay on welfare for relatively short periods—about 30 percent of those who went on welfare accumulated less than two years on the program (17 percent less than one year).

Women who bear their first child out of wedlock and while a teenager have been the subgroup most likely to go on welfare, and to accumulate the longest tenure on AFDC. Our estimates show that among a cohort of teenage unwed mothers, half have gone on welfare within the first two years of their first birth and eventually more than 80 percent have participated. Of those who have gone on welfare, half have stayed for more than five years, and 35 percent for more than seven years. This subgroup of the AFDC recipient population made up more than half of the AFDC caseload in 1996. Since teen unwed mothers on welfare have limited schooling and low cognitive achievement to begin with (in part a consequence of their early childbearing) and also acquire little work experience while on welfare, they are likely to experience difficulties supporting themselves and their children with a private sector job. They are the most likely group to come up against a five-year time limit and therefore will present the greatest problems for states seeking to move recipients into jobs.

There is a bright spot in this discouraging picture of teenage unwed mothers who go on welfare. A surprising percentage (about half) have left welfare for at least two years when observed about a decade after their first child's birth. Most work, but marriage appears to be the most effective way to attain a higher income. Those who married (53 percent) had a family income of $30,000 (1989 dollars), about three-fourths the income of women who bore their first child after marriage and never went on welfare. In contrast, those who left welfare but did not marry had an average total income of only $14,700.

Nonetheless, welfare participation, regardless of marital status or age at first birth, has a detrimental effect on the level of earnings attainable. Women who leave welfare have high rates of work participation, almost equaling those of women with children who have never been on welfare, but the earnings former welfare mothers can command remain substantially lower than those of other women. Although their earnings rise as they accumulate work experience, their low skills and lost years of work while on welfare perpetuate an earnings gap that is likely to be difficult to close.

The Effectiveness of Welfare-to-Work Programs

Chapter 4 addresses the question: how effective have been alternative types of programs in raising AFDC women's earnings and in reducing caseloads? Evidence is presented from research on three genres of programs: employment, education, and training for adult women with school-age children; education and other services for teenage mothers who were new AFDC recipients; and workfare. Results from the JOBS program are discussed in chapter 5.

One important caveat to this review is that the findings refer to programs implemented in an environment in which there was no limit on the time a women could remain on welfare. The conclusions about the programs' effectiveness may not necessarily apply to programs operated under an environment of welfare reform with a five-year lifetime limit.

Unfortunately, there is no evidence that any of the large number of education, employment, and training programs that have been offered or mandated for AFDC recipients since 1967 has had a significant impact on the duration of time spent on welfare. Although some programs have had positive effects on the employment and earnings of recipients, these effects have been too small and transitory to move significant numbers of recipients off welfare completely. These discouraging results apply to adult recipients as well as to young women enrolled in special programs for teenage AFDC mothers. Whether these programs would be more effective if combined with a mandatory welfare time-limit remains a question that cannot be answered with currently available data.

Workfare, although much discussed, has seldom been tried for single mothers on AFDC. Workfare is a program in which welfare recipients are mandated to perform an assigned job for a specified number of hours per week in return for welfare benefits. The empirical evidence on its effects is scanty, although one evaluation of such a program tried in Ohio did provide some evidence that it reduced the AFDC caseload. On theoretical grounds at least (see chapter 4), workfare constitutes a promising tool to be tried, particularly for women with school-aged children. On philosophical grounds, the idea of working for one's benefit may also help instill appropriate work attitudes among recipients.

In 1994, under the JOBS program, only 9 percent of all adult AFDC recipients were enrolled in a training program. The degree to which AFDC program administrators targeted AFDC recipients for training by assigning them *mandatory* status was no greater under JOBS than it was during the pre-JOBS era in the late 1980s. Since the new welfare legislation requires an increase in work activity participation to 25 percent of the adult caseload (rising to 50 percent), a large increase in resources could be required over current levels, especially for child care services. Such an expansion may not be feasible, at least in a short time period.

Prevention Versus Rehabilitation

It has proven to be extraordinarily difficult for any government program to transform the subgroup of recipients with multiple problems into workers who can earn a high enough income to support a family on their own and compete with the benefit offered to welfare recipients. Changes in incentives may improve the success rate of some traditional programs. But it is likely that a core group will continue to be difficult to reach.

For this core group it may be more fruitful for states to focus their efforts on measures aimed at preventing girls from starting on the path to welfare dependence in the first place. Such efforts could include narrowly targeted programs, such as teen pregnancy prevention programs and targeted employment programs. Unfortunately, the results of many such programs have not been very encouraging.[1] One of the exceptions is the JOBSTART program which while a training program appears to have reduced the probability of a first pregnancy and subsequent AFDC participation among teenage girls.

The fact of the matter, however, is that it has proven difficult for narrowly focused, short duration programs, such as the teen pregnancy prevention programs, to overcome the handicaps that often arise from growing up in a disadvantaged family and neighborhood.[2] Because of these larger conditioning factors it is important to turn to more fundamental institutions in our society to improve the upward mobility of disadvantaged groups.

School may be the institution best suited for addressing the problems underlying the skill deficiencies and attitudinal problems associated with welfare dependency. It is true that the performance of our schools, particularly those in poor and troubled neighborhoods, has been a long standing concern. In many cities, however, efforts are underway to provide new kinds of schooling opportunities for disadvantaged children, including special schools within the public school system, charter schools, publicly funded vouchers and privately funded scholarships. The ability to choose schooling alternatives, and features of the alternatives themselves, may encourage parents to become more involved in their children's development, a factor that is often lacking.

Moreover, the declining accessibility of welfare may give parents and their teenage children new incentives to utilize the schools if they are perceived as a way to improve incomes off welfare. It is hoped that the outcome of these efforts will be not only to raise academic performance but also to impart a positive influence on social attitudes and aspirations. Improvements in schooling opportunities, therefore, may in the long run help forestall the early childbearing and other behavior that often leads to future welfare dependence.

NOTES

1. See the review article on adolescent pregnancy prevention program by Moore et al. (1995).

2. Hill and O'Neill (1993) find a strong association between family and neighborhood characteristics while growing up and the likelihood of an out-of-wedlock birth and long-term welfare dependence.

Appendix A

Current Population Survey (CPS) and Caseload Measures of the Size of the AFDC Caseload

As illustrated in table A-1, major data sources do not agree on the overall number of AFDC families. The Current Population Survey (CPS) counts fewer families on welfare each year than the caseload data. Moreover, the difference between the AFDC BASIC caseload (total recipient units minus unemployed parent cases) and the CPS count of female-headed AFDC families widened between 1987 and 1992 when the CPS shows only two-thirds as many families as the caseload data.

Part of the discrepancy between the CPS and caseload measures arises because of differences in definition. The basic caseload data include a wider array of family types than the CPS series, which can be more cleanly restricted to female-headed families with children (no spouse present in the household). The AFDC caseload data, for example, contain cases without an adult recipient (although a caretaker adult is presumably present) and these *no adult* cases increased by 346,000 between 1987 and 1992—a 74 percent increase (column 3 of table A-1).[1] In 1992, *no adult* units accounted for close to half of the difference between the CPS and caseload measures of recipient families.

Insight into factors that might be responsible for the remaining CPS undercount is provided in a special study reported by Goudreau, Oberheu and Denton (1984) in which respondents to a follow-up survey conducted by the Census Bureau were matched with AFDC caseload records in several states. The study indicates that nonreporting of AFDC receipt to the Census Bureau was three times higher for those who were shown to have received benefits for a portion of the year compared to those receiving benefits throughout the period. A higher level of welfare nonreporting was also found for workers compared to nonworkers, and for married compared to nonmarried individuals. In all, it appears that the CPS may not seriously underreport the number of recipients who would be the primary targets for employment and training programs under welfare reform, since it is the transitory, short-term participants who are most likely to be missed by the CPS surveys.

We have also compared the size of the welfare population as measured by the CPS with that measured by the National Longitudinal Survey of Youth (NLSY), which is a very detailed survey with responses of relatively high quality and accuracy. Tables A-2 and A-3 show the results of this comparison. In table A-2, women ages 21-28 in 1986 are drawn from the CPS sample to correspond with the age range available in the NLSY cohort. (Table A-3 does the same for 1990 when the NLSY cohort was ages 25-32.) The female population counted by the CPS is larger than the NLSY population because the latter is a fixed cohort that can only diminish in size over time, while the CPS reflects a population expanded by immigrants who entered the country in large numbers during the 1980s, particularly in the age groups shown.

Despite differences in the construction of the two surveys, which can influence the identification of mother-child families, the two surveys depict approximately the same patterns for the cohorts examined.[2] The number of nonmarried mothers receiving welfare was about 940,000 in 1989 in the age group 25-32 years of age. This is a slightly lower number of recipients than was observed for this cohort in 1985 when they were ages 21-28; but since many more women became mothers over the four-year period these numbers also reflect a substantial decline in the *rate* of AFDC participation among single mothers as age increases. As women move into their late twenties and early thirties, a larger proportion of nonmarried mothers are divorced or separated and these women have considerably lower rates of welfare participation than women who bore their children out-of-wedlock.

It should be noted that the CPS measure of recipients is larger when receipt of *other welfare benefits* is counted as AFDC benefits. This more inclusive measure is likely to be more nearly the correct one. According to Goudreau, Oberheu and Vaughn (1984), a portion of the CPS undercount of welfare receipt is attributable to failure of the respondent to identify welfare benefits as AFDC when in fact that is what they are. We therefore have used the more inclusive definition in tables based on CPS data.

NOTES

1. As discussed in chapter 3, the passage of IRCA is believed to have made it easier for formerly illegal aliens to claim AFDC benefits for their children, although they themselves were given a five-year waiting period to qualify.

2. The CPS samples households, while the NLSY samples individuals. Until recently the CPS did not provide adequate information to correctly identify nonmarried mothers, if these mothers were heads of subfamilies rather than heads of primary families.

Table A.1 Comparison of CPS and Caseload Estimates of Single-Parent Families on AFDC, 1987-1992 (population in thousands)

	CPS data		AFDC caseload data			
Year	Female-headed families on AFDC	BASIC caseload, all families minus unemployed fathers	Units with "no adult" recipients	BASIC minus "no adult" units (2-3)	Families with one adult recipient	Total female adult recipients
	(1)	(2)	(3)	(4)	(5)	(6)
1987	2,578	3,548	361	3,187	3,044	3,344
1988	2,542	3,538	359	3,179	3,045	3,319
1989	2,373	3,578	407	3,178	3,076	3,285
1990	2,712	3,770	455	3,315	3,198	3,437
1991	2,938	4,107	558	3,549	3,483	3,712
1992	3,003	4,447	707	3,740	3,691	3,931
Percentage increase						
1987-92	16.5	24.3	73.7	17.4	21.3	17.6
1989-92	26.5	25.3	95.8	17.7	20.0	19.7

SOURCE: CPS data are from public use tapes of the Current Population Survey of March of the following year; AFDC caseload data are from the Office of Family Assistance, U.S. Department of Health and human Services.
NOTE: CPS data refer to the calendar year and caseload data to the fiscal year.

Table A.2 Comparison of AFDC Recipients in 1985 NLSY and CPS (Women Ages 21-28 in 1986)

	All women (000s)	Women with children		AFDC recipients		Recipients of AFDC and other welfare	
		(000s)	Percent of all women	(000s)	Percent of mothers	(000s)	Percent of mothers
NLSY, 1985							
Married	7,776	5,239	67.4	229	4.4	NA	
Never married	6,424	1,165	18.1	576	49.4	NA	
Other nonmarried	1,869	1,157	61.9	380	32.8	NA	
Total nonmarried	8,293	2,322	28.0	956	41.2	NA	
CPS, 1985							
Married	8,352	5,478	65.6	173	3.2	221	4.0
Never married	6,954	1,054	15.2	565	53.6	619	58.7
Other nonmarried	1,712	1,060	61.8	361	34.1	378	35.7
Total nonmarried	8,669	2,114	24.4	926	43.8	997	47.2

SOURCE: CPS data, see table A.1; NLSY data, NLSY microfiles.

Table A.3 Comparison of AFDC Recipients in 1989 NLSY and CPS (Women Ages 25-32 in 1990)

	All women (000s)	Women with children		AFDC recipients		Recipients of AFDC and other welfare	
		(000s)	Percent of all women	(000s)	Percent of mothers	(000s)	Percent of mothers
NLSY, 1989							
Married	9,505	7,184	75.6	178	2.5	NA	
Never married	3,780	1,039	27.5	443	42.6	NA	
Other nonmarried	2,653	1,835	69.2	498	27.1	NA	
Total nonmarried	6,433	2,874	44.7	941	32.7	NA	
CPS, 1985							
Married	10,412	7,768	74.6	167	2.1	195	2.5
Never married	4,516	1,054	23.3	462	43.8	475	45.1
Other nonmarried	2,452	1,668	68.0	444	26.6	469	28.1
Total nonmarried	6,968	2,722	39.1	906	33.3	944	34.7

SOURCE: CPS data, see table A.1; NLSY data, NLSY microfiles.

Appendix B

**Table B.1 Characteristics, Skills and Work Experience
of 22–29-Year-Old Women on AFDC in 1987, by Years
on Welfare Since 1978 (NLSY)**

	All women on AFDC in 1987	On AFDC 2 years or less	On AFDC more than 2 years	On AFDC 4 years or more
Percent Black	41.1	31.2	46.9	52.1
Percent Hispanic	10.5	7.3	10.9	12.1
Percent White	48.4	61.5	42.2	35.8
Percent teen at first birth	56.6	38.5	65.5	73.6
Percent out-of-wedlock first birth	61.6	40.3	70.6	75.9
Percent southern	24.9	27.0	23.8	22.7
Number of children:				
in year entered AFDC	1.39	1.55	1.31	1.32
in 1988	2.12	1.85	2.26	2.36
Percent high school dropout:				
in year went on AFDC	47.5	22.7	52.7	57.5
in 1988	32.9	18.6	38.0	50.1
AFQT percentile (mean)	27.1	34.0	24.5	22.6
Percent went on AFDC within 2 years of first birth	45.5	29.8	57.4	59.6
Percent worked before AFDC	75.2	95.5	73.9	65.6
Weeks worked by working women before going on AFDC	120	179	75.0	59.8

(continued)

Table B.1 (continued)

	All women on AFDC in 1987	On AFDC 2 years or less	On AFDC more than 2 years	On AFDC 4 years or more
Total months on AFDC (mean)	48.1			
Sample size	570	134	392	291
Weighted population (thousands)	1,050	328	723	506

References

Bane, Mary Jo and David T. Ellwood. 1993. "The Dynamics of Dependence: The Routes to Self-Sufficiency." Report prepared for the U.S. department of Health and Human Services by Urban Systems Research and Engineering.

Becker, Gary. 1981. *Treatise of the Family.* Cambridge, MA: Harvard University Press.

Blank, Rebecca M. 1989. "Analyzing the Length of Welfare Spells," *Journal of Public Economics* 39, 3 (August): 245-273.

Bloom, Dan, V. Fellerath, David Long, and R.G. Woods. 1993. "LEAP: Attendance Among Teen Parents." Manpower Demonstration Research Corporation May.

Case, George, et al. 1993. "JOBSTART: Final Report on a Program for School Dropouts." Manpower Demonstration Research Corporation, October.

Economic Report of the President. 1967, 1976, 1980 and 1994.

Ellwood, David T. 1986. "Targeting 'Would be' Long-Term Recipients of AFDC." Mathematica Policy Research.

Friedlander, D., J. Riccio, and S. Freedman. 1993. "GAIN: Two Year Impacts in Six Counties." Manpower Demonstration Research Corporation, May.

Friedlander, D., and Gayle Hamilton. 1993. "The Saturation Work Initiative Model (SWIM) in San Diego." Manpower Demonstration Research Corporation, July 1993.

Gabe, Thomas. 1992. "Demographic Trends Affecting AFDC Caseload Growth." Paper presented at the annual meetings of APPAM, Denver, October.

General Accounting Office. 1991. "Welfare to Work." GAO Report to the Committee on Finance, U.S. Senate, GAO/HRD-91, No. 6, September.

_____. 1992. "Welfare to Work: States Serve Least Job-Ready While meeting JOBS Participation Rates." U.S. GAO/HRD 93-2, Washington, November.

_____. 1993. "States Move Unevenly To Serve Teen Parents In Jobs." U.S. GAO/HRD 93-74, July.

Goudreau, Karen, Howard Oberheu, and Vaughn Denton. 1984. "An Assessment of the Quality of Survey Reports of Income from the Aid to Families with Dependent Children (AFDC) Program," *Journal of Business & Economic Statistics*, 2, 2 (April): 179-186.

Greenberg, David, and Michael Weisman. 1992. "What Did the Work Demonstrations Do?" University of Wisconsin—Madison, Institute for Research on Poverty, Discussion Paper No. 969-92, April.

Grossman, J., R. Maynard, and J. Roberts. 1985. "Reanalysis of the Effects of Selected Employment and Training Programs for Welfare Recipients." Mathematica Policy Research.

Haveman, Robert H., and John K. Scholz. 1994-1995. "The Clinton Welfare Reform Plan: Will It End Poverty as We Know It?" *FOCUS* 16, 2 (Winter): 1-11.

Hill. M. Anne, and June O'Neill. 1995. *Underclass Behaviors in the U.S.: Measurement and Analysis of Determinants.* New York: Center for the Study of Business and Government, Baruch College, CUNY.

Hymowitz, Kay S. 1994. "Up The Up Staircase," *City Journal* (Spring): 31-39.

Janzen, Frederick K., and Mary Jane Taylor. 1991. "Emergency Welfare Work and Employment: An Independent Evaluation of Utah's Emergency Work Program." Final report, Social Research Institute, Graduate School of Social Work, University of Utah, June.

Katz. Jeffrey. 1996. "Welfare Overhaul Law." Congressional Quarterly 54, 38 (September): 2696-2705.

Kemple, Jane J., and Joshua Haimson. 1994. "Florida's Project Independence." Manpower Demonstration Research Corporation, January.

Ketron, Inc. 1980. *The Long Term Impact of WIN II: A Longitudinal Evaluation of the Employment Experience of Participants in the Work Incentive Program.* Philadelphia: Ketron.

Leigh, Duane E. 1993. "Did FIP Increase The Self-Sufficiency of Welfare Recipients in Washington State? Evidence From the FIP Data Set." University of Wisconsin-Madison, Institute For Research on Poverty, Discussion Paper No. 1812-93, August.

Long, S.K., and D.A. Wissoker. 1992. *Short-Run Net Impacts of the Washington State Family Independence Program (FIP).* Washington, DC: Urban Institute, June.

Lynch. John M., and Dave M. O'Neill. 1973. *Poverty and Public Policy.* Special Analysis Series, American Enterprise Institute.

Maynard, Rebecca (Ed.). 1993. *Building Self-Sufficiency Among Welfare Dependent Teenage Parents, Lessons from the Teenage Parent Demonstration.* Princeton, NJ: Mathematica Policy Research.

Mincer, J., and H. Ofek. 1982. "Interrupted Work Careers: Depreciation and Restoration of Human Capital," *Journal of Human Resources* 17 (Winter): 3-24.

Mincer, J., and S. Polachek. 1974. "Family investments in Human Capital: Earnings of Women," *Journal of Political Economy*, Supplement 82: 576-108.

Moffitt, Robert. 1992. "Incentive Effects of the U.S. Welfare System: A Review," *Journal of Economic Literature* 30 (March): 1-61.

_____. 1996. "The Effect of Welfare on Marriage and Fertility: What Do We Know and What Do We Need to Know?" Paper prepared for Conference on the Effect of the Welfare System on the Family and Reproductive Behavior, National Academy of Sciences.

Moore, K.A., B.W. Sugland, C. Blumenthal, D. Glei, and N. Snyder. 1995. *Adolescent Pregnancy Prevention Programs: Interventions and Evaluations.* Washington, DC: Child Trends Inc.

O'Neill, June. 1990a. *Work and Welfare in Massachusetts: An Evaluation of the ET Program.* Boston: Pioneer Institute for Public Policy Research.

_____. 1990b. "The Role of Human Capital in Earnings Differences Between Black and White Men," *Journal of Economic Perspectives* 4, 4 (Fall): 25-45.

_____. 1993. "Can Work and Training Programs Reform Welfare?" *Journal of Labor Research* 14, 3 (Summer): 265-281.

O'Neill, June A., Laurie J. Bassi, and Douglas A. Wolf. 1987. "The Duration of Welfare Spells," *Review of Economics and Statistics* 69: 241-249.

O'Neill, June A., Douglas A. Wolf, Laurie J. Bassi, and Michael T. Hannan. 1984. *An Analysis of Time on Welfare.* Washington, DC: Urban Institute.

Peskin, Janice. 1993. "Forecasting AFDC Caseloads, with an Emphasis on Economic Factors." Congressional Budget Office Staff Memorandum, July.

Peskin, Janice, J. Topogna, and D. Marcotte. 1992. "How the Economy Affects AFDC Caseloads." Paper presented at the annual meetings of APPAM, Denver, October.

Polit, D.F., J.C. Quint, and J.A. Riccio. 1988. *The Challenge of Serving Teenage Mothers.* New York: Manpower Demonstration Research Corporation, October.

Quint, J.C., B. Fink, and S. Rowser. 1991. *New Chance: Implementing a Comprehensive Program for Disadvantaged Young Mothers and Their Children.* New York: Manpower Demonstration Research Corporation, December.

Quint, Janet C., Judith S. Musick, and Joy A. Ladner. *Lives of Promise, Lives of Pain: Young Mothers After New Chance.* New York: Manpower Demonstration Research Corporation, January.

Rector, Robert. 1993. "Welfare Reform, Dependency Reduction and Labor Market Entry," *Journal of Labor Research* 14, 3 (Summer): 283-297.

Romero, Carol J. 1994. "JTPA Programs and Adult Women on Welfare: Using Training to Raise AFDC Recipients Above Poverty." Research Report No. 93-01, National Commission for Employment Policy, October.

Schiller, Brady, and Neil C. Brasher. 1993. "Effect of Workfare Saturation on AFDC Caseloads," *Contemporary Policy Issues* 11 (April): 39-49.

U.S. Bureau of the Census. 1992. "Poverty in the United States: 1992." Current Population Reports, Series P60-185.

INDEX

About the Institute

The W.E. Upjohn Institute for Employment Research is a nonprofit research organization devoted to finding and promoting solutions to employment-related problems at the national, state, and local level. It is an activity of the W.E. Upjohn Unemployment Trustee Corporation, which was established in 1932 to administer a fund set aside by the late Dr. W.E. Upjohn, founder of The Upjohn Company, to seek ways to counteract the loss of employment income during economic downturns.

The Institute is funded largely by income from the W.E. Upjohn Unemployment Trust, supplemented by outside grants, contracts, and sales of publications. Activities of the Institute are comprised of the following elements: (1) a research program conducted by a resident staff of professional social scientists; (2) a competitive grant program, which expands and complements the internal research program by providing financial support to researchers outside the Institute; (3) a publications program, which provides the major vehicle for the dissemination of research by staff and grantees, as well as other selected work in the field; and (4) an Employment Management Services division, which manages most of the publicly funded employment and training programs in the local area.

The broad objectives of the Institute's research, grant, and publication programs are to: (1) promote scholarship and experimentation on issues of public and private employment and unemployment policy; and (2) make knowledge and scholarship relevant and useful to policymakers in their pursuit of solutions to employment and unemployment problems.

Current areas of concentration for these programs include: causes, consequences, and measures to alleviate unemployment; social insurance and income maintenance programs; compensation; workforce quality; work arrangements; family labor issues; labor-management relations; and regional economic development and local labor markets.

DATE DUE

JA 20 '99			

DEMCO 38-297